A field guide to the

Birds of Sri Lanka

A field guide to the Birds of Sri Lanka

Sarath Kotagama & Prithiviraj Fernando

The Wildlife Heritage Trust of Sri Lanka

To Namalee, Tharani and Nisha

A field guide to the birds of Sri Lanka

Sarath Kotagama & Prithiviraj Fernando

ISBN 955-9114-07-7

Typeset in Palatino by Iris Colour Graphics,
95 Cotta Road, Colombo 8, Sri Lanka.

Colour separation by Iris Colour Graphics,
95 Cotta Road, Colombo 8, Sri Lanka.

Printed by Gunaratne Offset Limited.

CONTENTS

ACKNOWLEDGEMENT

This field guide has been a dream for many years. The original text was completed almost ten years ago, but without the availability of a suitable artist to do the plates, and a sympathetic publisher, the material remained in manuscript form. The field book became a reality with Dr Prithiviraj Fernando agreeing to do the plates and the Wildlife Heritage Trust agreeing to publish it. We are grateful to Rahula Perera, Mahendra Siriwardena, Vimukthi Weeratunga, P. B. Karunaratne, Upali Ekanayake and Rex de Silva for their contributions. To Nisha and Namalee for their patience and encouragement. Finally, to all the bird watchers who continuously encouraged our efforts.

Sarath Kotagama

INTRODUCTION

Birdwatching is a hobby that can give immense pleasure to anybody. In addition, it is a hobby that makes you truly appreciate the wonders of nature. It provides not only intellectual satisfaction but also pleasant recreation and exercise. It needs patience, self discipline and a degree of tolerance. It is often the case that long treks into the wild result with no significant observations. These are all part of the challenge of birdwatching.

Birdwatching can also improve one's knowledge of the environment, animal behaviour and biological relationships. Many theories in the fields of animal behaviour, ecology and evolution, to mention a few, have been tested through observations of birds. The observation of birds does not demand sophisticated instrumentation. The most important quality needed by any serious birdwatcher is a methodical approach. Essentially, a systematic effort to observe, record, interpret and disseminate the information gathered on birds, their habits and habitats.

Birdwatching involves three basic steps:

    identification of birds

    recording of observations

    reporting and disseminating the findings

The majority of birdwatchers center their interest on recording bird sightings. This is the major objective of amateur birdwatching. In this Guide, we pay particular attention to helping to achieve this objective. With the help of this book, you should be able to put a name with reasonable accuracy on any bird you are likely to see in Sri Lanka.

IDENTIFICATION OF BIRDS

Parts of birds commonly used for identification

A knowledge of the names of the external parts of birds (topography) is necessary for their identification and description (see Figures 1 & 2). These figures refer to the most widely used names assigned to the parts of birds, including waders.

Figure 1.

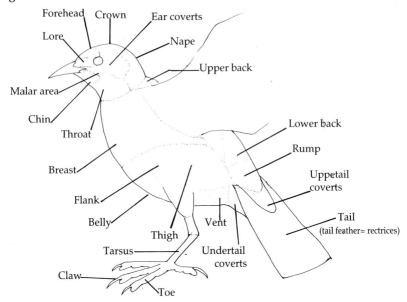

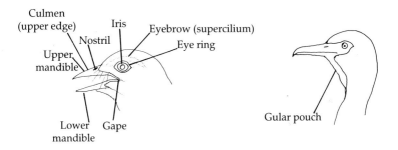

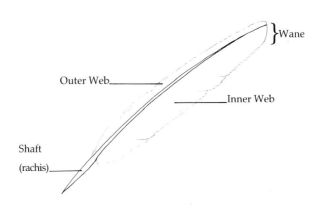

Figure 2.
Forest bird

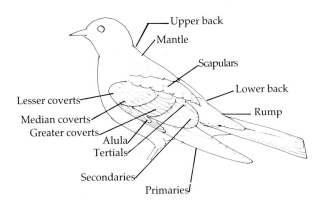

Upper back
Mantle
Scapulars
Lower back
Rump
Lesser coverts
Median coverts
Greater coverts
Alula
Tertials
Secondaries
Primaries

Wader

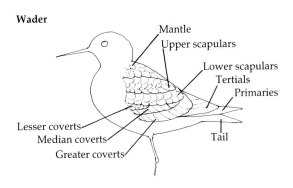

Mantle
Upper scapulars
Lower scapulars
Tertials
Primaries
Lesser coverts
Median coverts
Greater coverts
Tail

Upper wing (left side)

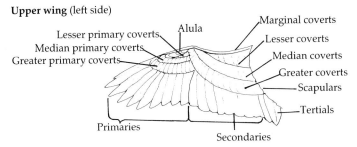

Lesser primary coverts
Median primary coverts
Greater primary coverts
Alula
Marginal coverts
Lesser coverts
Median coverts
Greater coverts
Scapulars
Tertials
Primaries
Secondaries

Underwing (left side)

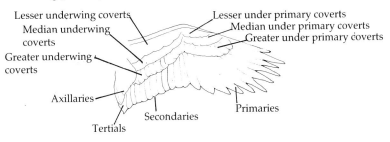

Lesser underwing coverts
Median underwing coverts
Greater underwing coverts
Lesser under primary coverts
Median under primary coverts
Greater under primary coverts
Axillaries
Tertials
Secondaries
Primaries

BIRD NAMES

All living things known to science are given scientific names. Better known species (which include most birds) also have vernacular names by which they are popularly known. Scientific names, of course, are written in Latin and remain valid everywhere in the world.

The scientific names used in this book are based on "Distribution and Taxonomy of Birds of the World" by Sibley and Monroe (1990), in keeping with the general acceptance by the Oriental Bird Club and Birdlife International. Names that are different to those used in Phillips (1978) have been marked with an asterisk (*). However, the classification adopted by us does not follow Sibley and Monroe. This is in view of the still unsettled condition of their work (see Ibis 1994: (136) 12-18). Instead we have used the standard sequence of "Peters checklist of the birds of the world". The nomenclature and distinguishing characters for subspecies follows Ali and Ripley (1969).

Vernacular names tend to change from place to place, even within a country. In order to bring some uniformity to the vernacular names of birds, they have been standardised. The English vernacular names used in this text are those given in Sibley and Monroe (1990). However, in order not to confuse or make it difficult for older birdwatchers, the present vernacular names in use (Phillips, 1978) have been given in parantheses in the descriptive text, where the change is very drastic. Sinhala names given here are those developed and published by Perera and Kotagama (1983) with some modifications. The etymological method for the Sinhala names adopted by Perera and Kotagama (1983) has enabled names to be coined for new sight records that had no previous Sinhala names. This approach enables the amateur to master very easily the scientific names of birds which has to be the ultimate goal of any serious birdwatcher.

IDENTIFICATION FEATURES

EXTERNAL ANATOMY

Profile. Several bird groups (e.g. pelicans, flamingos) have distinctive profiles. This is probably the most fundamental feature used in bird identification. Typical profiles for families are given in the descriptive text.

Size. One of the most important features for the identification of a bird is its size. It is useful, when describing an unfamiliar bird, to compare it to the size of a familiar one. Birds of the same size are assumed to be of the same shape unless stated that they are slimmer, taller, longer-necked and so on, than the one being compared. The usefulness of this method depends on the reader being familiar with the reference bird used.

It is useful therefore to have a standard set of well-known birds for the purpose of size comparison. Two sets have been proposed by Kotagama (1986), for this purpose, one for forest species and the other for wetland species. Here we include slightly modified versions for those two (Figures 3 & 4).

Figure 3. Forest birds for size comparison.

8 cm: Pale-billed Flowepecker

10 cm: Scaly-breasted Munia

15 cm: House Sparrow

20 cm: Red-vented Bulbull

23 cm: Common Mynah

33 cm: Dometic Pigeon

48 cm: Large-billed Crow

70 cm: Junglefowl ♂ (♀ 35 cm)

51-71 cm: Serpent-Eagle

102-117 cm:Peafowl ♀ and ♂ without train. 250 cm: ♂ with train

Figure 4. Wetland birds for size comparison.

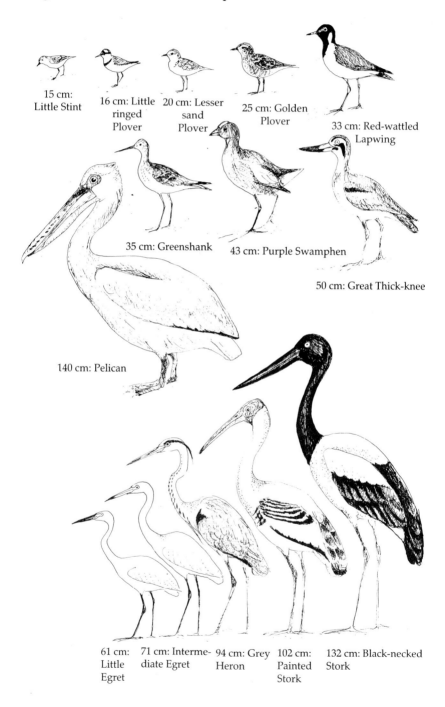

15 cm: Little Stint

16 cm: Little ringed Plover

20 cm: Lesser sand Plover

25 cm: Golden Plover

33 cm: Red-wattled Lapwing

35 cm: Greenshank

43 cm: Purple Swamphen

50 cm: Great Thick-knee

140 cm: Pelican

61 cm: Little Egret

71 cm: Intermediate Egret

94 cm: Grey Heron

102 cm: Painted Stork

132 cm: Black-necked Stork

Figure 5. Some bird species that can be identified by the beak.

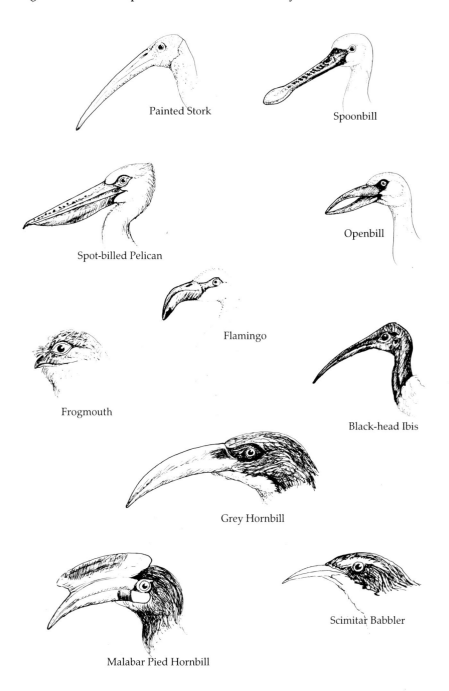

Painted Stork

Spoonbill

Spot-billed Pelican

Openbill

Flamingo

Frogmouth

Black-head Ibis

Grey Hornbill

Malabar Pied Hornbill

Scimitar Babbler

Figure 6. Some common bird groups that can be identified by the beak.

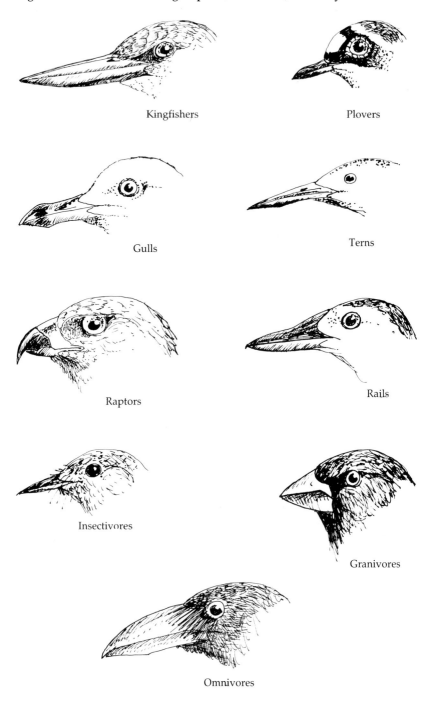

Kingfishers

Plovers

Gulls

Terns

Raptors

Rails

Insectivores

Granivores

Omnivores

14

Figure 7. Some foot types of birds.

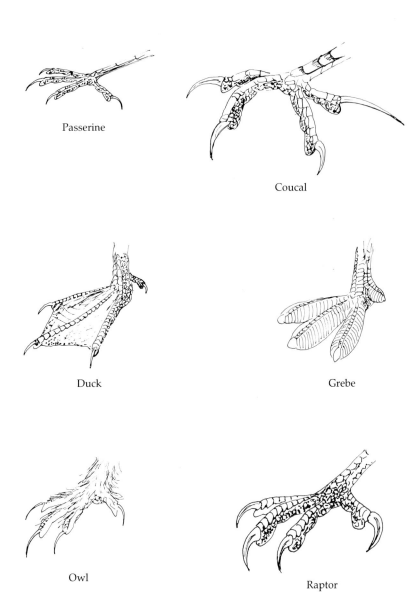

Passerine

Coucal

Duck

Grebe

Owl

Raptor

Figure 8. Some tail shapes.

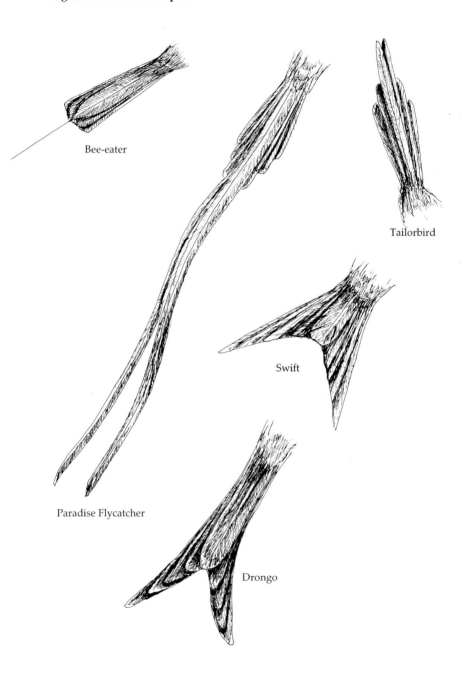

Bee-eater

Tailorbird

Swift

Paradise Flycatcher

Drongo

Figure 9. Some wing shapes.

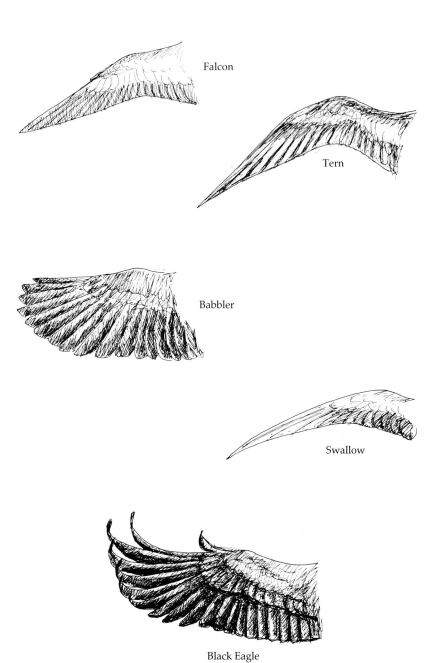

Falcon

Tern

Babbler

Swallow

Black Eagle

Figure 10. Some special head structures in birds.

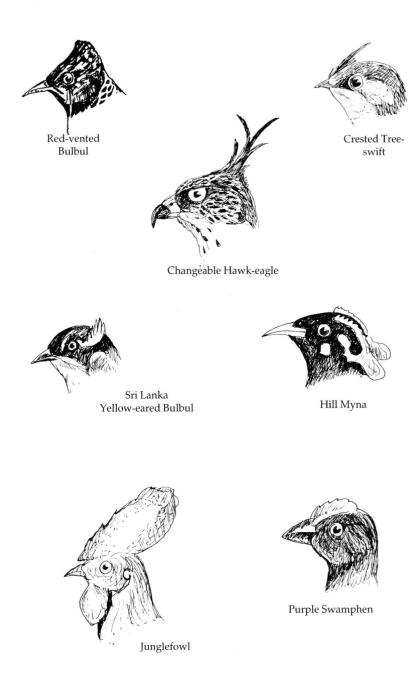

Red-vented
Bulbul

Crested Tree-
swift

Changeable Hawk-eagle

Sri Lanka
Yellow-eared Bulbul

Hill Myna

Junglefowl

Purple Swamphen

Figure 11. Some behavioural activities helpful in identification.

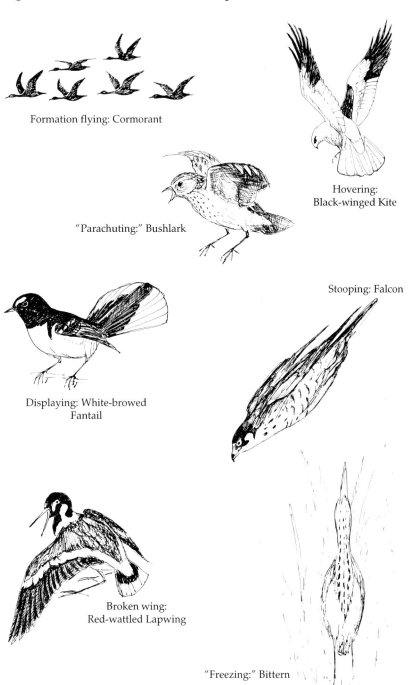

Formation flying: Cormorant

"Parachuting:" Bushlark

Hovering:
Black-winged Kite

Displaying: White-browed
Fantail

Stooping: Falcon

Broken wing:
Red-wattled Lapwing

"Freezing:" Bittern

Figure 12. Flight types.

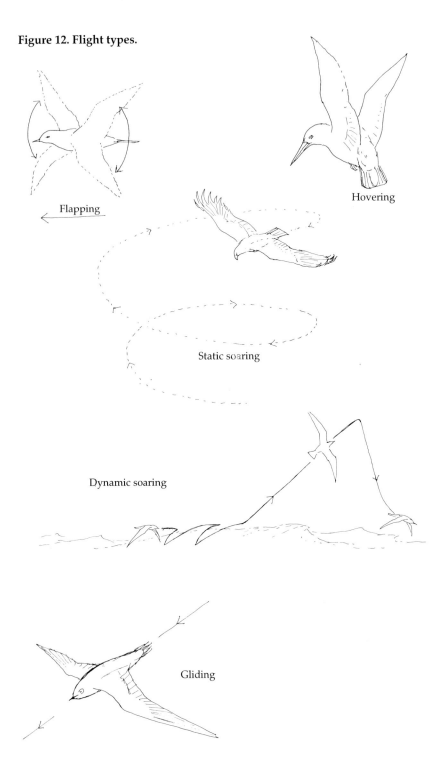

Flapping

Hovering

Static soaring

Dynamic soaring

Gliding

Beak. The shape and size of a bird's beak (bill) indicates to a great extent the nature of its food and manner of feeding. Different beak structures have enabled birds to exploit different habitats and fit into a wide range of niches. Figure 5 shows distinct beak shapes that help identify some bird species, while Figure 6 shows shapes that help identify some common groups. In some cases the sexes can be differentiated by the beak shape and size.

Legs and feet. Legs and feet do not show as much diversity as the beak. Yet their length, color and structure assist in identification (Figure 7). The most important field characters are usually the color and length of the legs (particularly in the case of wetland birds).

Tail. A bird's tail is often more visible than its legs. Its main function is to steer the bird during flight and to assist in landing. Tail shape helps identify some species (Figure 8). The tail is sometimes used for displaying as in the White-browed Fantail and this too, is important in identification.

Wings. The shape and size (length and width) of a bird's wings are good indicators of the nature of flight, flight speed and distance. The most common wing shape is that of the passerines (e.g. the crow), but some characteristic shapes and sizes enable groups of birds to be identified easily (Figure 9).

Special parts. Some birds possess special structures or parts of the body that are distinctive, often extensions of feathers or skin. The crest is one such feature (Figure 10). Some of these plumage characters develop only during the breeding season, but in Sri Lankan birds this is relatively rare. Among skin extensions are wattles (e.g. Red-wattled Lapwing) and lappets (e.g. grackles).

ACTIVITY AND BEHAVIOR

Instinctive behaviour or habits are good clues for the identification of several groups or species of birds (e.g. the way flycatchers pick their prey or the peculiar dance of the White-browed Fantail). There are several other more subtle, but yet characteristic mannerisms such as the stalking habit of egrets and herons, hunting habits of owls or birds of prey, the bobbing of the tail by sandpipers and tail wagging by wagtails. The nature of movement on the ground (such as hopping or walking) and flight are other useful characters. Some examples are given in Figure 11 and a few of the more important groups are discussed below.

Flight. Bird flight can be very broadly categorised into four types: flapping, hovering, soaring and gliding (Figure 12).

Flapping flight. This is the most common flight type among birds and involves the use of the wing to generate both propulsion and lift.

Hovering. As shown by humming birds or sometimes by Sunbirds and Pied Kingfishers. This involves active flapping of the wings in a slightly different way to that of flapping flight, enabling the bird to remain stationary in mid air. This action is referred to as active hovering. Passive hovering, is often shown by birds of prey such as Black-winged Kite and Brahminy Kite to name two birds that characteristically are able to hover over a spot on the ground by gliding into the wind.

Figure 13. Diagrammatic representation fo flight styles.

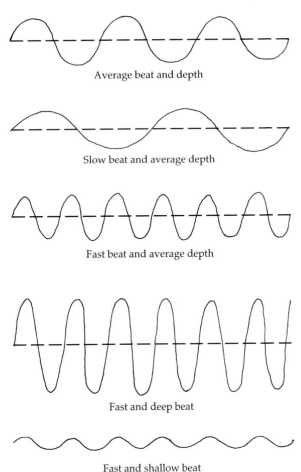

Average beat and depth

Slow beat and average depth

Fast beat and average depth

Fast and deep beat

Fast and shallow beat

Variations in flight pattern

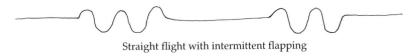

Straight flight with intermittent flapping

Undulating flight with flapping at the bottom of the trough

Soaring. Terrestrial birds, especially birds of prey (e.g. vultures) are static soarers. In Sri Lanka, static soaring is shown by all the large birds of prey, storks and pelicans. Making use of thermal updrafts, they soar high into the sky and glide down to enter another updraft if they desire to keep aloft. If not, they settle on the ground or on a perch. As they are dependent very much on thermal updrafts, these birds are active mostly during mid-day and less so in the morning and evening. They are common close to rocky areas or open lands that heat up rapidly to create thermal updrafts. This is the main reason for birds of prey being a common nuisance in airports.

Marine birds are typically good dynamic soarers (e.g. boobies), they make use of the differential wind speeds above the ocean to help them remain in flight for very long spells, sometimes for many years.

Gliding. This is a rather uncommon flight style. To glide, the bird must first reach some attitude, and descend without flapping its wings.

Unfortunately most birds do not adhere strictly to any one of the four flight types listed above. Not only do we often see combinations of flapping, gliding and soaring, but flapping alone is subject to much variation (frequency and amplitude of the wing beat).

The symbolic representation on Figure 13 can be used to describe the flight styles of most birds for the purpose of identification.

Calling. The act of calling or singing is a good feature for identification. Some birds call more during the breeding season than at other times. The koel is known to call frequently during the months of March and April (during the time of the Sri Lankan new year) and has the common Sinhala name "Avurudu koha" (avurudu = new year).

The stance and position of a bird when calling or singing is useful for identification. The Magpie Robin will sing from the highest position in its territory, the skylark stands very upright when it sings, or sings while flying down. Many such observations for different species can be used for their identification.

Feeding. The feeding behaviour of birds varies considerably, but in certain instances it can be used to pin down an identification. It is particularly useful for group identifications in most instances. The flycatching of flycatchers, feeding mechanisms of pipits, plovers, curlew sandpipers, spoonbills and sunbirds are good examples. The feeding methods of birds of prey too may differ in the way they catch the prey. Falcons kill their prey in flight, most others pounce on unsuspecting prey.

Moving. Apart from flying, birds move about on the ground, in the canopy and in water using their feet. This varies from hopping to walking to swimming. The way they do this in the course of their daily activities such as feeding is often different, thus helping in their identification.

Breeding. Breeding involves many activities including the selection of mates, courtship, nest building, incubation and care of young. Observations of these could help in the identification of some species. It is in fact a feature used even for species identification in taxonomy. The bill-rattling of storks, the dancing of bulbuls and magpies, the social preening of crows and babblers are a few examples of distinctive breeding behavior.

SPECIAL FEATURES

Calls and songs

Birds have the ability to communicate using sound, and for this purpose they make use of calls or songs generated by a vocal apparatus known as the syrinx. In a few special cases, the sound is produced by mechanical means such as beating wings (e.g. the jungle fowl) or drumming the beak against the bole of a tree (e.g. woodpeckers). The call or song is generaly specific to each species except in the case of a small number of species which have the ability to mimic the calls of other birds or to learn new vocalizations altogether. An example would be the chloropsis, which mimics the call of the Shikra, and the White-vented Drongo which mimics cats or sometimes other birds. Generally, the call or song is a very good means to make a positive identification of a birds. Naturally, this requires some experience and training. Hearing a call or a song of a positively identified bird is the best way to learn this, and assistance from people familiar with bird calls hastens the process.

Unfortunately, there is no universally accepted notation for bird calls, but some authors have attempted to represent the sounds by similar-sounding words. Some examples from G.M. Henry's "A guide to the Birds of Ceylon" are given below:

Small Flowerpecker (Pale-billed Flowerpecker)	-	"constantly uttered, tlik, tlik...."
Red-vented Bulbul	-	"The notes consist of sprightly calls, some of which suggest the words "ginger beer" and "sweet potatoes...."
Common southern Nightjar	-	"like the tapping of a glass marble dropped from a height of a yard or so on to a cement floor...."

One dufficulty with such descriptions is that one has to be familiar with the pronounciation of the words to imagine the call or song.

Another approach to this problem has been to use musical notes or symbols, making it necessary that the reader be familiar with musical notation. In recent times sonograms have been used for depicting and analyzing calls and songs. Tape recordings of common bird calls are now becoming an important accessory to bird identification and probably represents the best teaching approach in this area.

A call is generally considered to be a short burst of sounds while a song is an assemblage of such calls in a sequence to provide a continuous roll of sound in a specific way. The distinction between calls and songs is not always clear.

Color. While color is the most extensively used field character for the identification of birds, it is also the most unreliable. Color is dependent on available light and certain colors appear best only when the light is incident at certain angles or intensities. Colors appear different in morning, mid-day and afternoon light. This is especially important with colors that are dependent on the property of refracted light, such as glossy or metallic effects. The brightness of the color and the color itself may depend on the angle from which one views the bird. Looking into the sun, the color of a bird will appear dark.

Color also depends on humidity and the wetness of feathers. The colors of dry feathers are different to those of wet feathers. Atmospheric humidity too, plays an important role in the appearence of color. The difference in the color of birds in the dry zone and the wet zone is often for this reason. Differences in the intensity or shade of a color are considered by some taxonomists as adequate to seperate subspecies, for example in the Brown-capped Babbler and the Tailor-bird.

It is well known that in many birds (e.g. the flamingo), color is dependent on diet. It is probably for this reason that birds in captivity tend to be less bright than those in the wild.

Description of color by means of words presents obvious difficulties. The various shades of green for example, are numerous and description in words can be very difficult. Common objects in use have been used as references for colors, e.g. orange and chestnut, but requires familiarity with the objects, which may differ in availability between societies. In this text, all color descriptions are based on well understood colors and their combinations. Chestnut will be reddish-brown, brown being the major color with a tinge of red.

Though color can be quite confusing and sometimes misleading, we are very dependent on color for the identification of birds. Therefore it is hoped that the color plates will help in this effort, but one must be aware of their limitations.

Field characters. Some of the above features by themselves or in combination, are definitive features useful for positive identification of birds in the field. These are often referred to as field characters. e.g. the position of a particular color pattern:

- rose ring around the neck of the Rose-ringed Parakeet;
- the red shoulder patch of the Alexandrine Parakeet;
- the white eye-brow of the White-browed Prinia;
- the red face of the Red-faced Malkoha;
- the white tips to the tail feathers of the Blue Magpie;
- the red patch on the forehead of the Crimson-fronted Barbet;
- the white rump of the Shama;
- the wing bar of the Serpent-Eagle;

The list is obviously extensive and the main field charater for each species is given in the text.

Habitat. Most birds are associated with certain habitats and observations should always take note of this. Habitat associations could be obvious (e.g. fruit trees or flowers associated with certain birds). Observations should always be accompanied by habitat notes as most birds are habitat-specific. (Finding a bird in the "wrong" place can also be a good indicator. e.g., crows are normally associated with human habitations and finding a colony of crows in a wildlife reserve, for example, indicates that it is a disturbed habitat).

Indirect features. There are a few indirect features that can be used for the identification of birds. These are based on material or structures the bird produces, such as nests or food pellets. Feathers may also be considered in this category. Nests are often specific to certain groups of birds, and in certain instances to certain species. Some examples are given in Figure 14. Food pellets are mostly from birds such as owls and bee-eaters. In most cases the species cannot be easily identified but the taxonomic group can be identified. Feathers too, can be useful, especially as some are very specific in their patterns.

GETTING STARTED

Every good birdwatcher should be armed with a note book, which is considered to be an essential requirement. Field notes in the case of a bird you have not seen before, should include a sketch of the bird with as many details as possible. This is a habit that one needs to cultivate early, as a sketch assists memory and helps prevent one's imagination taking root in the identification of birds. Very often, descriptions "off the head" are not accurate and one tends to visualize and imagine colors and shapes on being prompted.

Binoculars. Though not essential, binoculars make birdwatching easier, enabling one to see details of birds at a distance. One of the difficult but challenging tasks in bird watching is to try to approach as closely as possible the bird you are observing. Attempt this and see for yourself that often the bird sees you before you see it, or it will notice you approaching and fly away. Developing the skill of stalking a bird is a very challenging task by itself and could be very enjoyable. To go a step further, and if you are determined to make bird watching a life-long hobby, it is as well to obtain binoculars.

Selection of binoculars should be done with care. Choose a reputed brand. There are two basic forms of binoculars. Roof prism and porro prism. Roof prism binoculars have the advantage of more compact size but are more expensive. Cheep roof prisms tend to be less satisfactory than a porro prism pair of similar price. The magnification of the binoculars is given in the form 8X, 7X, 10X etc. Larger magnifications look attractive, but require very steady hands and reduce the field of vision. They are thus almost useless in forests and with birds that are often moving. Mounted on a tripod, they can be useful for observing birds such as waders, but this involves additional cost and further limits mobility. It is best to select a pair of all-purpose binoculars that can be used under average conditions. The recommended magnifications are from 7 to 10. Magnifications higher than 10 are not really practical.

The second "rating" given on binoculars (along with   magnification) is the diameter of the objective lens. The "light gathering" power of binoculars is

Figure 14. Some indirect features.

Paradise Flycatcher nest

Sunbird nest

Tailorbird nest

Munia nest

Figure 15. A page from the field note book.

1. Date : 20129304 (date ; month ; year ; record number)

2. Time : 0930 (time according to the 24 hr. system. Midnight = 2400 hrs.)

3. Location : Sinharaja Forest , Research Station , near ' Cobra ' Bridge .

4. Habitat : Near a flowing stream , on a stick beside the stream .

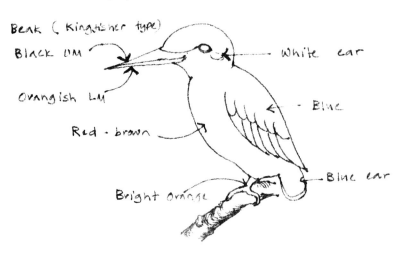

Beak (Kingfisher type)
Black UM
White ear
Orangish LM
Blue
Red - brown
Blue ear
Bright orange

Size : about 6 cm .

5. Habits : Perched very erect ; raises head up and down from time to time .

determined by dividing the diameter of the objective lens (given usually in millimetres) by the magnification. The higher the value the better light gathering power. For example 7X50 binoculars are good for making observations under low light conditions. Another criterion is the aperture size (the small circle seen when looking through the ocular lens-the lens closest to the eye with the binoculars held a few inches away from the eyes). The larger the size of the apperture the better the quality of the binoculars. 8X40 binoculars are considered a good compromise of all these factors.

In addition to these factors, the quality of the prisms, the glass used in the lenses and the refracting surfaces will effect the quality of the image. If you can afford it, waterproof, sealed binoculars are a worth while investment. If not, try and keep your binoculars in a dessicator when not in use. (due to the high humidity in a tropical climate like Sri Lanka, fungus tends to grow on the inside surfaces of the lenses). Cleaning affected lenses tends to damage the coating, so prevention is better than the cure!

Warning. Do not select binoculars primarily because they are cheap. Poor optics can harm your sight and cause persistent headaches.

Attitude. One has to cultivate a few important habits in order to become a good birdwatcher: patience, silence, controlling emotions, sharing information and the ability to work in small groups. Seeking birds can be a very frustrating exercise, especially in heavily forested areas. Hour after hour could be spent without any useful sightings of birds. The ability to maintain interest for long periods of time thus becomes a cornerstone in birdwatching. Birdwatching also requires an ability to walk for long periods of time. Interest in the outdoors and walking can help tremendously in your interst in birdwatching. Finally, going out to watch birds, you also need to be properly attired. Avoid bright colors or white. "Earthy" colors such as browns and greens are best. Birds need peace as much as we do, so avoid disturbing them

USING THE FIELD GUIDE

This field guide consists of three sections.

Color plates
Descriptive text and
Text for pelagic species and Incidentals.

Given below are examples of the format of the text for each section.

The color plates illustrate 239 species which include most of the commoner species and a few rare species. The birds have not been drawn to scale, but their size (tip of beak to end of tail) is stated in the text.

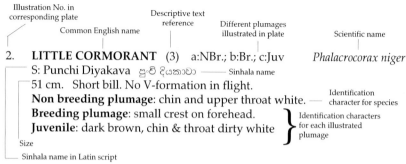

Illustration No. in corresponding plate
Common English name
Descriptive text reference
Different plumages illustrated in plate
Scientific name

2. **LITTLE CORMORANT** (3)   a:NBr.; b:Br.; c:Juv   *Phalacrocorax niger*
S: Punchi Diyakava පුංචි දියකාවා —— Sinhala name
51 cm. Short bill. No V-formation in flight.
Non breeding plumage: chin and upper throat white. — Identification character for species
Breeding plumage: small crest on forehead. } Identification characters for each illustrated plumage
Juvenile: dark brown, chin & throat dirty white
Size
Sinhala name in Latin script

The descriptive text is arranged according to the classification. A typical silouhelte for families is given as a quick reference guide. In addition to the 239 species in the color plates, this section contains descriptions of a further 93 species which are mostly rare. A black and white illustration is provided for them.

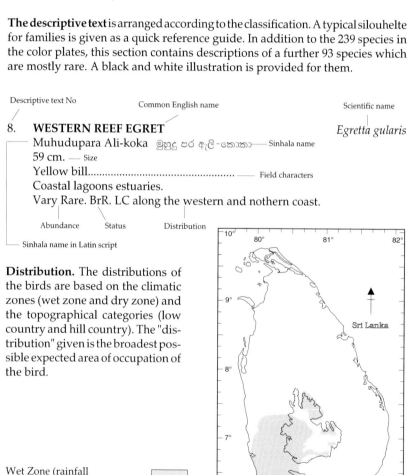

Descriptive text No
Common English name
Scientific name

8.   **WESTERN REEF EGRET**   *Egretta gularis*
Muhudupara Ali-koka මුහුදු පර ඇලි-කොකා —— Sinhala name
59 cm. — Size
Yellow bill.. — Field characters
Coastal lagoons estuaries.
Vary Rare. BrR. LC along the western and nothern coast.

Abundance   Status   Distribution
Sinhala name in Latin script

Distribution. The distributions of the birds are based on the climatic zones (wet zone and dry zone) and the topographical categories (low country and hill country). The "distribution" given is the broadest possible expected area of occupation of the bird.

Wet Zone (rainfall > 2000mm per year)

Elevation over 500m

N.b. The comment on abundance refers to the abundance of the bird within its area of distribution in Sri Lanka.

The text for pelagic species (sea birds) and incidentals is also arranged according to the same classification used elsewhere in the text. It follows the same format as the descriptive text and in addition, gives the reference to literature on incidentals and sight records.

ABBREVIATIONS AND SYMBOLS USED IN THE TEXT

♂	-	Male
♀	-	Female
Juv	-	Juvenile
Br	-	Breeding
NBr	-	Non-breeding
LC	-	Low Country
HC	-	Hill Country
DZ	-	Dry Zone
WZ	-	Wet Zone
BrR	-	Breeding Resident
CBCN	-	Ceylon Bird Club Notes
*	-	indicates that the scientific name used here differs from that used by Phillips (1978)
Size	-	refers to the straight line length from the tip of the beak to the end of the tail

BIRD ORGANIZATIONS IN SRI LANKA

1. Ceylon Bird Club
    P.O. Box 11,
    Colombo.

2. Field Ornithology Group of Sri Lanka
    C/o Department of Zoology,
    University of Colombo,
    Colombo 3.

Plate 1

1. **SPOT-BILLED PELICAN** (2)   *Pelecanus philippensis*
   S: Alu Pasthuduwa   අළු පැස්තුඩුවා
   140 cm. Long, large bill with a large gular pouch.

2. **LITTLE CORMORANT** (3) a:NBr.; b:Br.; c:Juv.   *Phalacrocorax niger*
   S: Punchi Diyakava   පුංචි දියකාවා
   51 cm. Short bill. No V-formation in flight.
   Non breeding plumage; Chin and upper throat white.
   Breeding plumage; Small crest on forehead.
   Juvenile; Dark brown, chin and throat dirty white.

3. **GREAT CORMORANT** (5) Br.   *Phalacrocorax carbo*
   S: Maha Diyakava   මහ දියකාවා
   91 cm. White cheeks, yellow throat.
   Breeding plumage; large white patch on flanks, white feathers on nape and hind neck.

4. **INDIAN CORMORANT** (4)
   a:NBr.; b:Br.; c:Juv.   *Phalacrocorax fuscicollis*
   S: Hadapalu Diyakava   හැඩපළු දියකාවා
   65 cm. Long slender bill. V-formation during flight.
   Non breeding plumage; white border to gular pouch.
   Breeding plumage; white feather tuft behind eye, white speckles on head and neck.
   Juvenile; Upperparts dark brown. Underparts dirty white.

5. **ORIENTAL DARTER** (6) NBr,;   *Anhinga melanogaster*
   S: Ahikava   අහිකාවා
   90 cm. Long, slender, brown neck with dagger-like bill.

6. **LITTLE GREBE** (1) a:NBr.; b:Br.; c:Juv.   *Tachybaptus ruficollis**
   S: Heen Gembithuruwa   හීන් ගෙඹිතුරුවා
   25 cm. Whitish patch at gape.
   Breeding plumage; reddish-brown throat and fore neck.
   Non breeding plumage; whitish throat.
   Juvenile; Striped upperparts.

Plate 2

1. **INTERMEDIATE EGRET** (12)
   a:NBr.; b:Br.   *Mesophoyx intermedia**
   S: Sudu Madi-koka   සුදු මැදි-කොකා
   71 cm. **Non-breeding plumage;** yellow bill often with dusky tip.
   Breeding plumage; plumes on upper breast and lower back.

2. **LITTLE EGRET** (7)   a:NBr.; b:Br.   *Egretta garzetta*
   S: Kuda Ali-koka   කුඩා ඇලි-කොකා
   61 cm. Bill and legs black. Feet yellow.
   Breeding plumage; plumes on nape, lower breast and back.

3. **GREAT EGRET** (11)   a:NBr.; b:Br.   *Casmerodius albus**
   S: Maha Sudu-koka   මහ සුදු-කොකා
   94 cm. **Non breeding plumage;** yellow bill.
   Breeding plumage; plumes on lower back only.

4. **CATTLE EGRET** (13)   a:NBr.; b:Br.   *Bubulcus ibis*
   S: Gava-koka   ගව-කොකා
   51 cm. Chin prominent. Often associated with ungulates.
   Non-breeding plumage; Completely white.
   Breeding plumage; Head neck and back, golden-brown.

5. **GREY HERON** (9)   *Ardea cinerea*
   S: Alu Koka   අළු කොකා
   94 cm. Black line running from eye, through nape to occipital region.

6. **PURPLE HERON** (10)   *Ardea purpurea*
   S: Karaval Koka   කරවැල් කොකා
   79 cm. Black crown. Reddish-brown neck with dark stripe.
   Dark underparts.

7. **STRIATED HERON** (15)   *Butorides striatus*
   S: Kuda pala Kana-koka   කුඩා පලා කණ-කොකා
   52 cm. Grey-green plumage with dark upperparts.

Plate 3

1. **INDIAN POND HERON** (14) a:NBr.; b:Br.   *Ardeola grayii*
    S: Kana-koka තණ-කොකා
    46 cm. Dark body contrasting with white of wings and tail in flight.
    Breeding plumage; Intensity of purple on back increases.
    Well developed head plumes.

2. **BLACK-CROWNED NIGHTHERON** (16)
    a:NBr.; b:Juv   *Nycticorax* nycticorax
    S: Ra-koka රෑ-කොකා
    56 cm. Crown and upper back black. White head plumes.
    Juvenile; Brown with whitish spots above and brown streaks below.

3. **BLACK BITTERN** (20) ♂   *Ixobrychus flavicollis**
    S: Kalu Mati-koka කළු මැටි-කොකා
    58 cm. Orange-brown streak from chin to upper breast.

4. **CINNAMON BITTERN** (19) ♂   *Ixobrychus cinnamomeus*
    S: Rathu-dumburu Mati-koka රතු-දුඹුරු මැටි-කොකා
    38 cm. Very prominent white chin.

5. **YELLOW BITTERN** (18) ♂   *Ixobrychus sinensis*
    S: Kaha Mati-koka කහ මැටි-කොකා
    16 cm. Cap and tail black.

6. **WHITE-BREASTED WATER HEN** (77)   *Amaurornis phoenicurus*
    S: Laya sudu Korawakka ලය සුදු කොරවක්කා
    33 cm. Face and breast white.

7. **PURPLE SWAMPHEN** (81)   *Porphyrio porphyrio*
    S: Nil Kithala නිල් කිතලා
    43 cm. Bill, legs and head shield, red.

8. **COMMON MOORHEN** (82)   *Gallinula chloropus*
    S: Galinuwa ගැලිනුවා
    33 cm. Black plumage with white line along flanks.

Plate 4

1. **WOOLY-NECKED STORK** (23)   *Ciconia episcopus*
   S: Padili Manawa   පාදිලි මානාවා
   91 cm. Black body, wings and crown. White neck and belly.

2. **EURASIAN SPOONBILL** (28)   a:NBr.; b:Br.   *Platalea leucorodia*
   S: Handi Alawa   හැඳි ආළාවා
   84 cm. Flattened spoon-shaped bill.
   Breeding plumage: Crest and reddish-yellow band on upper breast.

3. **PAINTED STORK** (21)   Br.   *Mycteria leucocephala**
   S: Lathuvakiya   ලතුවැකියා
   102 cm. Naked head and yellow decurved bill.

4. **BLACK-HEADED IBIS** (27)   Br.   *Threskiornis melanocephalus*
   S: Sudu Da-koka   සුදු දෑ-කොකා
   76 cm. Naked black neck and head. Black long, decurved bill.

5. **GLOSSY IBIS** (26)   NBr.   *Plegadis falcinellus*
   S: Silutu da-thuduwa   සිලුටු දෑ-තුඩුවා
   68 cm. Appears black (but plumage glossy green with bronze
   and purple reflections). Head and neck region speckled appearance.

6. **BLACK-WINGED STILT** (121)   *Himantopus himantopus*
   S: Piyapath kalu Ipalpava   පියාපත් කළු ඉපල්පාවා
   38 cm. Distinct, red, long legs.

7. **ASIAN OPEN-BILL** (22)   Br.   *Anastomus oscitans*
   S: Vivara-thuduwa   විවර-තුඩුවා
   81 cm. Open space between mandibles.

8. **PHEASANT-TAILED JACANA** (84)
   a:♂ Br.; b:♀ / ♂ NBr.   *Hydrophasianus chirurgus*
   S: Savulpenda Diyasana   සැවුල්පෙඳ දියසැනා
   30 cm. **Male (breeding):** long blackish-brown tail.
   Female and non-breeding male: Hind neck duller. No elongate tail
   feathers.

Plate 5

1. **LESSER ADJUTANT** (25)   *Leptoptilos javanicus*
   S: Bahuru-manawa බහුරු-මානාවා
   115 cm. Neck and head unfeathered. Bill yellowish.

2. **GREATER FLAMINGO** (29)   *Phoenicopterus ruber**
   S: Seeyakkaraya සීයක්කාරයා
   127 cm. Extremely long neck and legs. Bent bill.

3. **BLACK-NECKED STORK** (24)
   a:♂ b:♀   *Ephippiorhynchus asiaticus**
   S: Ali-manawa අලි-මානාවා
   132 cm. Neck and lower back region black.
   Male: Dark brown irides.
   Female: Yellow irides.

4. **LESSER WHISTLING-DUCK** (31)   *Dendrocygna javanica*
   S: Kuda Thumba-seruwa කුඩා තුඹ-සේරුවා
   40 cm. Brownish plumage. Dark brown cap.

5. **NORTHERN PINTAIL** (37) a:♂ Br.; b:♀   *Anas acuta*
   S: Ul-penda Seruwa උල්-පෙඳ සේරුවා
   75 cm. (Male) 56cm. (Female) **Male**: white streak on side
   of neck and long tail.
   Female: mottled brown. Slender, pointed tail.

6. **GARGANEY** (38) a:♂ Br.; b:♀   *Anas querquedula*
   S: Gargeni Seruwa ගාගනී සේරුවා
   38 cm. Broad white eyebrow.

7. **COTTON PYGMY-GOOSE** (33) a:♂ b:♀   *Nettapus coromandelianus*
   S: Mal-sera මල්-සේරා
   33 cm. **Male:** blackish crown and black collar.
   Female: dark line through eye and white eyebrows.

Plate 6

1. **SHIKRA** (55) ♂   *Accipiter badius*
   S: Kurulugoya කුරුළුගොයා
   30-35 cm. **Male:** reddish-brown narrow bars on breast and belly.

2. **BLACK-WINGED KITE** (44)   *Elanus caeruleus*
   S: Pathanukussa පතනුකුස්සා
   33 cm. Black shoulder patch. Hovers frequently.

3. **CRESTED SERPENT-EAGLE** (49)   *Spilornis cheela*
   S: Sarapukussa සරපුකුස්සා
   51-71 cm. Yellowish spots on upperparts and white spots
   on underparts. Prominent wing bar in flight.

4. **ORIENTAL HONEY-BUZZARD** (43)   *Pernis ptilorhyncus*
   S: Siluvathi Bambarukussa සිළුවැති බඹරුකුස්සා
   51 cm. Unevenly spaced dark bands on tail. Head pigeon-like
   from the side.

5. **CHANGEABLE HAWK-EAGLE** (61)   *Spizaetus cirrhatus*
   S: Kondakussa කොණ්ඩකුස්සා
   69 cm. Crest and slim body.

6. **MOUNTAIN HAWK-EAGLE** (62)   *Spizaetus nipalensis*
   S: Kandukara Bondakussa කඳුකර කොණ්ඩකුස්සා
   72 cm. (Male). 80cm (Female). Brownish bars on lower breast and belly.

7. **BLACK EAGLE** (58)   *Ictinaetus malayenisis*
   S: Kalukussa කළුකුස්සා
   69 cm. Black plumage with lores, area around eye and feet yellow.

Plate 7

1. **COMMON KESTREL** (63) ♂   *Falco tinnunculus*
   S: Parisarikussa පරිසාරිකුස්සා
   34 cm. Hovers frequently.
   Male: upper-parts reddish-brown with black spots.

2. **BRAHMINY KITE** (46)   *Haliastur indus*
   S: Bamunu Piyakussa බමුණු පියාකුස්සා
   45 cm. Brownish-red and white plumage.

3. **GREY-HEADED FISH-EAGLE** (48)   *Ichthyophaga ichthyaetus*
   S: Waw Masukussa වැව් මසුකුස්සා
   70 cm. Lower belly, under tail coverts and basal 2/3 of tail white.

4. **WHITE-BELLIED FISH- EAGLE** (47)   *Haliaeetus leucogaster*
   S: Sethodara Diyakussa සේතෝදර දියකුස්සා
   71 cm. White head and under parts.

5. **PIED HARRIER** (52) ♂   *Circus melanoleucos*
   S: Kalu-sudu Harikussa කළු-සුදු හැරිකුස්සා
   43-45 cm. **Male:** black and white plumage.

6. **WESTERN MARSH HARRIER** (50) ♀/Juv   *Circus aeruginosus*
   S: Waguru Harikussa වගුරු හැරිකුස්සා
   48-56 cm. **Female and juvenile:** dark brown plumage with cap,
   throat and shoulders buff color.

Plate 8

1. **SRI LANKA JUNGLE FOWL** (72) a:♂ b:♀   *Gallus lafayetii*
    S: Lanka Wali kukula   ලංකා වලි-කුකුලා
    70 cm. (Male). 35cm. (Female).
    Male: Crimson comb with a central yellow patch and long tail feathers.
    Female: upperparts brown, vermiculated with black.

2. **BARRED BUTTON-QUAIL** (74) a:♂ b:♀   *Turnix suscitator*
    S: Bola-watuwa   බෝල-වටුවා
    16 cm. A dark brown bird with barred plumage.
    Male: sides of the head white, with bold black barring on breast.
    Female: black chin, throat and centre of breast.

3. **BLUE-BREASTED QUAIL** (69) a:♂ b:♀   *Coturnix chinensis*
    S: Laya Nilwatuwa   ළය නිල්වටුවා
    15 cm. **Male:** throat and upper breast with black and white
    markings; lower breast and flanks slaty blue.
    Female: brown breast; flanks with blackish bars.

4. **INDIAN PEAFOWL** (73) a:♂ b:♀   *Pavo cristatus*
    S: Monara/Sebeda   මොණරා/සෙබඩ
    102-117 cm (without train). Characteristic crest feathers on head.
    Male: brilliant, glistning-blue neck and breast.
    Female: no train, brown and white plumage.

5. **SRI LANKA SPURFOWL** (71)
    a:♂ b:♀   *Galloperdix bicalcarata*
    S: Lanka Haban-kukukla   ලංකා හබන-කුකුලා
    33 cm. Naked red orbital skin.
    Male: Contrasting black and white spots on underparts.
    Female: dull brownish red.

Plate 9

1. **EURASIAN THICK-KNEE** (124)   *Burhinus oedicnemus*
S: Kuda Golu-kalikaya   තුඩා ගොළු-කාලිකයා
40 cm. Characteristic head shape with large yellow
"goggle" eyes. White wing band.

2. **GREAT THICK-KNEE** (125)   *Burhinus recurvirostris**
S: Maha Golu-kalikaya   මහ ගොළු-කාලිකයා
50 cm. Large yellow iris. Large heavy bill.

3. **GREY PLOVER** (87)   a:NBr.; b:Br.   *Pluvialis squatarola*
S: Alu Maha-oleviya   අළු මහ-ඔලෙවියා
28 cm. Greyish upperparts. Black axillaries in flight.

4. **PACIFIC GOLDEN PLOVER** (86)
a:NBr.; b:Br.   *Pluvialis fulva**
S: Ran Maha-oleviya   රන් මහ-ඔලෙවියා
25 cm. Mottled brown upperparts. Dark spot on earcoverts.

5. **GREATER SAND PLOVER** (91)
a:NBr.; b:Br.   *Charadrius leschenaultii*
S: Maha vali Oleviya   මහ වැලි ඔලෙවියා
23 cm. Bill longer than lesser sand plover (6).

6. **LESSER SAND PLOVER/MONGOLIAN PLOVER** (90)
a:NBr.; b:Br.   *Charadrius mongolus*
S: Kuda vali Oleviya   කුඩා වැලි ඔලෙවියා
20 cm. Legs dark brown or dark grey.

7. **KENTISH PLOVER** (89)   a:NBr.; b:Br.   *Charadrius alexandrinus*
S: Kentiya Oleviya   කෙන්ටිය ඔලෙවියා
18 cm. No breast band. Black patch on side of breast.

8. **LITTLE RINGED PLOVER** (88)
a:NBr.; b: Br.   *Charadrius dubius*
S: Heen mala Oleviya   හීන් මාල ඔලෙවියා
16 cm. Upper breast and upper back encircled by a black band.
Eye ring, legs, and sometimes base of lower mandible, yellow.

Plate 10

1. **EURASIAN CURLEW** (103)   *Numenius arquata*
   S: Kalikaya කාලිකයා
   59 cm. Long, down-curved bill (10-15 cm).

2. **WHIMBREL** (102)   *Numenius phaeopus*
   S: Vimburaliya විඹුරළියා
   43 cm. Long, down-curved bill (8-10 cm).
   Crown broadly striped with black and white.

3. **PIED AVOCET** (122)   *Recurvirostra avosetta*
   S: Avasattha අවසැත්තා
   43 cm. Slender black up-curved bill.

4. **PINTAIL SNIPE** (97)   *Gallinago stenura**
   S: Penda ul Kaswatuwa පෙඳ උල් කැස්වටුවා
   25 cm. Very narrow white band on rear edge of secondaries.

5. **RED-WATTLED LAPWING** (94)   *Vanellus indicus*
   S: Rath karamal Kirala රත් කරමල් කිරලා
   33 cm. Prominent red wattles; yellow legs.

6. **YELLOW-WATTLED LAPWING** (93)   *Vanellus malabaricus*
   S: Kaha karamal Kirala කහ කරමල් කිරලා
   28 cm. Yellow wattles and yellow legs.

7. **ORIENTAL PRATINCOLE** (127) Br.   *Glareola maldivarum**
   S: Peradige Javalihiniya පෙරදිග ජවලිහිණියා
   25 cm. Tern-like. Forked tail.

8. **SMALL PRATINCOLE** (128)   *Glareola lactea*
   S: Kuda Javalihiniya කුඩා ජවලිහිණියා
   18 cm. Tern-like. White wing-band in flight. Square-cut tail.

Plate 11

1. **EURASIAN OYSTERCATCHER** (85) *Haematopus ostralegus*
   S: Bolugulla බොලුගුල්ලා
   45 cm. Distinctive red bill and pinkish legs; black and white plumage.

2. **RUFF** (119) a:NB.; b:Br., displaying male. *Philomachus pugnax*
   S: Lovichchiya ලොවිච්චියා
   Male 30 cm; female 25 cm. Very similar to redshank,
   but upperparts with a distinctly flaked appearence.
   Leg color may vary from yellow to red.
   Inflight: white oval patches on side of upper tail coverts.

3. **BLACK-TAILED GODWIT** (100) NBr. *Limosa limosa*
   S: Penda kalu Gohoduvittha පෙඳ කළු ගොහොඳුවිත්තා
   40 cm. Gently sloping forehead. Straight black bill.
   Black band at tip of tail.

4. **BAR-TAILED GODWIT** (101) NBr. *Limosa lapponica*
   S: Iri penda Gohoduvittha ඉරි පෙඳ ගොහොඳුවිත්තා
   38 cm. Steep forehead. Slightly up-curved bill. Tail narrowly barred.

5. **COMMON GREENSHANK** (107) NBr. *Tringa nebularia*
   S: Palapa Silibilla පලාපා සිලිබිල්ලා
   35 cm. White forehead. Bill, long and slightly upturned.

6. **COMMON REDSHANK** (105) NBr. *Tringa totanus*
   S: Rathpa Silibilla රත්පා සිලිබිල්ලා
   28 cm. Yellowish-red legs and red base of bill.

7. **RUDDY TURNSTONE** (112)
   a:NBr.; b:Br.; ♂. *Arenaria interpres*
   S: Galharawanna ගල්හරවන්නා
   20 cm. Short, conical, black, slightly upturned, bill.
   Short yellowish-red legs. Characteristic lever-like action when feeding.

Plate 12

1. **GREEN SANDPIPER**   (108) a:NB.; b:Br.   *Tringa ochropus*
   S: Kola Silibilla   කොළ සිලිබිල්ලා
   24 cm. Upper parts blackish (brown glossed with bronze green).

2. **WOOD SANDPIPER** (109) NBr.   *Tringa glareola*
   S: Wana Silibilla   වන සිලිබිල්ලා
   23 cm. Upperparts dark brown speckled with white.

3. **MARSH SANDPIPER** (106) NBr.   *Tringa stagnatilis*
   S: Waguru Silibilla   වගුරු සිලිබිල්ලා
   25 cm. Very white plumage. Straight, very thin bill. Long legs.

4. **TEREK SANDPIPER** (110) NBr.   *Tringa cinerea**
   S: Terek Silibilla   ටෙරෙක් සිලිබිල්ලා
   25 cm. Slender, upturned black bill with yellow base.
   Short reddish-yellow legs.

5. **CURLEW-SANDPIPER**   (117) a:NBr.; b:Br.   *Calidris ferruginea*
   S: Kalika Hinna   කාලිකා හින්නා
   21 cm. Decurved black bill. Short legs.

6. **COMMON SANDPIPER** (111) NBr.   *Tringa hypoleucos*
   S: Podu Silibilla   පොදු සිලිබිල්ලා
   20 cm. Brown breast patch and white shoulder mark. Tail bobbing.

7. **LITTLE STINT** (114) a:NB.; b:Br.   *Calidris minuta*
   S: Heen Hinna   හීන් හින්නා
   15 cm. Very active. Short black bill and legs.

8. **LONG-TOED STINT**   (116) a:NBr.; b:Br.   *Calidris subminuta*
   S: Padangili diga Hinna   පාදැඟිලි දිග හින්නා
   17 cm. Distinct eyebrow.
   Crown streaked with black. Yellowish-green legs.

9. **TEMMINCK'S STINT** (115) NBr.   *Calidris subminuta*
   S: Temminck hinna   ටෙම්ක් හින්නා
   15 cm. Indistinct eyebrow. Breast light brownish grey.
   Legs greenish or yellowish, occasionally blackish.
   White outer tail feathers.

Plate 13

1. **BROWN-HEADED GULL** (130) a:NBr.; b: Br.   *Larus brunnicephalus*
   S: Hisa dumburu Galuviya   හිස දුඹුරු ගලුවියා
   45 cm. Dark, blackish, vertical crescent mark behind eye.
   In flight: "mirror" at tip of black primaries large.

2. **GREAT BLACK-HEADED GULL** (129)
   a:NBr.; b:Br.   *Larus ichthyaetus*
   S: Maha hisa-kalu Galuviya   මහ හිස-කළු ගලුවියා
   69 cm.Black patch around eye.
   In flight: tips of primaries white with inner black line.

3. **GULL-BILLED TERN** (131) a:NBr.; b:Br.   *Sterna nilotica**
   S: Galu-hota Muhudu-lihiniya   ගලු-හොට මුහුදු-ලිහිණියා
   38 cm. Short, stout, black bill. **Breeding plumage**: black cap on head.

4. **GREAT CRESTED TERN** (134)   *Sterna bergii*
   S: Maha konda Muhudu-lihiniya   මහ කොණ්ඩ මුහුදු-ලිහිණියා
   45 cm. Large greenish yellow bill. Black crest.

5. **CASPIAN TERN** (132)   *Sterna caspia**
   S: Caspiyanu muhudu-lihiniya   කැස්පියානු මුහුදු-ලිහිණියා
   54 cm. Large red bill. **Breeding plumage**: black cap.

6. **ROSEATE TERN** (136) a:NBr.; b:Br.   *Sterna dougallii*
   S: Arunuvan Muhudu-lihiniya   අරුණුවන් මුහුදු-ලිහිණියා
   33 cm. Tail deeply forked. Tail projects well beyond folded wing.
   Breeding plumage: pinkish tinge on underparts.

7. **WHISKERED TERN** (142) a:NBr.; b:Br.   *Chlidonias hybridus*
   S: Kangul-lihiniya   කානුල්-ලිහිණියා
   28 cm. Head with a small black cap with a streaky
   appearance on forehead.

8. **WHITE-WINGED TERN** (143) a:NBr.; b:Br.   *Chlidonias leucopterus**
   S: Piyapath sudu Kangul-lihiniya   පියාපත් සුදු කානුල්-ලිහිණියා
   25 cm. Complete white collar. Shallow tail fork.
   Breeding plumage: black head, body and wing lining.

9. **LITTLE TERN** (138) a:NBr.; b:Br.   *Sterna albifrons**
   S: Kuda Muhudu-lihiniya   කුඩා මුහුදු-ලිහිණියා
   23 cm. Black bill. Dusky red legs.
   Breedingplumage: Reddish yellow bill and legs.

10. **BRIDLED TERN** (140) a:NBr.; b:Br.   *Sterna anaethetus*
    S: Piyapath dumburu Muhudu-lihiniya   පියාපත් දුඹුරු මුහුදු-ලිහිණියා
    42 cm. Long, white outer tail feathers. Well-forked tail.
    Breeding plumage: brown parts of head black.

Plate 14

1. **SRI LANKA WOOD-PIGEON** (145)   *Columba torringtoni*
    S: Lanka Maila-goya   ලංකා මයිල-ගොයා
    35 cm. A black and white chess board pattern on hindneck,
    below which is a shiny reddish area.

2. **ORANGE-BREASTED GREEN-PIGEON** (150)
    a:♂ b:♀   *Treron bicincta*
    S: Laya ran Batagoya   ළය රන් බටගොයා
    25 cm. Tail blue-grey. **Male**: purplish-red-yellow breast.

3. **POMPADOUR GREEN-PIGEON** (151) a:♂ b:♀   *Treron pompadora*
    S: Pompadura Batagoya   පොම්පදෝර බටගොයා
    25 cm. Tail blue-grey with the middle tail feathers greenish.
    Male: maroon (dark purple) back.

4. **GREEN IMPERIAL-PIGEON** (153)   *Ducula aenea*
    S: Maha Neela-goya   මහ නිල-ගොයා
    43cm. Upper parts metallic bronzy-green. Red eyes and feet.

5. **EMERALD DOVE** (149) ♂   *Chalcophaps indica*
    S: Neela-kobeyiya   නිල-කොබෙයියා
    25 cm. White forehead.

6. **SPOTTED DOVE** (146)   *Streptopelia chinensis*
    S: Alu Kobeyiya   අළු කොබෙයියා
    30 cm. Spotted ashy-blue plumage with black and white
    pattern on hind neck.

Plate 15

1. **LITTLE GREEN BEE-EATER** (202)   *Merops orientalis*
   S: Palavan Binguharaya පලාවන් බිඟුහරයා
   20 cm. Chin and throat blue, central tail-feathers elongate.

2. **BLUE-TAILED BEE-EATER** (203)   *Merops philippinus*
   S: Pendanil Binguharaya පෙඳනිල් බිඟුහරයා
   30 cm. Yellow chin. Throat reddish-brown. Central tail feathers elongate.

3. **CHESTNUT-HEADED BEE-EATER** (204)   *Merops leschenaulti*
   S: Pinguhis Binguharaya පිඟුහිස් බිඟුහරයා
   17 cm. Crown, hind neck and upperback bright reddish-brown.
   Central tail feathers not produced outwards.

4. **PLUM-HEADED PARAKEET** (157)
   a:♂ b:♀   *Psittacula cyanocephala*
   S: Pandu Girawa පඬු ගිරවා
   34 cm. **Male:** rose pink head and red patch on shoulder.
   Female: dull grey-violet head and yellow collar. No red shoulder patch.

5. **SRI LANKA HANGING PARROT** (154) ♂   *Loriculus beryllinus*
   S: Lanka Giramaliththa ලංකා ගිරාමලිත්තා
   14 cm. Small, short square tail.
   Male: small blue patch on throat.

6. **ALEXANDRINE PARAKEET** (155) a:♂ b:♀   *Psittacula eupatria*
   S: Labu Girawa ලබු ගිරවා
   51 cm. Red patch on shoulder.
   Male: rose-pink half-collar.

   LAYARD'S PARAKEET (158)
   a:♂ b:♀   *Psittacula calthorpae*
   S: Lanka alu Girawa ලංකා අළු ගිරවා
   30 cm. Short tail. **Male:** red bill.
   Female: duller and with black bill.

8. **ROSE-RINGED PARAKEET** (156) a:♂ b:♀   *Psittacula kramerii*
   S: Rana Girawa රණ ගිරවා
   40 cm. **Male:** rose-pink half-collar.
   Female: lacks collar but has indistinct emerald green ring
   around the neck.

Plate 16

1. **PIED CUCKOO** (159)   *Oxylophus jacobinus**
   S: Gomara Konda-koha   ගෝමර කොණ්ඩ-කොහා
   35 cm. Prominent black crest. Black and white bird with a long tail.

2. **GREY-BELLIED CUCKOO** (165)
   a:♂ b:♀ -hepatic phase.   *Cacomantis passerinus**
   S: Lathoni Pingu-koha   ලතෝනි පිඟු-කොහා
   21 cm. Red irides.
   Male and grey phase female; Grey head, throat and upper breast.
   Red or 'hepatic' phase female; brown color.

3. **RED-FACED MALKOHA** (170)
   ♂   *Phaenicophaeus pyrrhocephalus*
   S: Watha rathu Malkoha   වත රතු මල්කොහා
   45 cm. Bright red facial patch.

4. **ASIAN KOEL** (167)   a:♂ b:♀   *Eudynamys scolopacea*
   S: Koha   කොහා
   43 cm. Irides red. **Male:** shining black plumage.
   Female: brown, profusely spotted and barred with white.

5. **BLUE-FACED MALKOHA** (168)   *Phaenicophaeus viridirostris*
   S: Watha nil Malkoha   වත නිල් මල්කොහා
   39 cm. Long graduated tail tipped with white.
   Blue naked patch round eyes.

6. **SRI LANKA GREEN-BILLED COUCAL** (172)
                        Centropus chlororhynchus
   S: Lanka bata Ati-kukula   ලංකා බට ඇටි-කුකුළා
   43 cm. Black plumage. Purplish gloss on neck,
   bright reddish brown wings. Green bill.

7. **GREATER COUCAL** (171)   *Centropus sinensis*
   S: Ati-kukula   ඇටි-කුකුළා
   48 cm. Black plumage with reddish brown wings. Black bill.

Plate 17

1. **BROWN FISH-OWL** (178)   *Ketupa zeylonensis**
   S: Dumburu Kevul-bakamuna දුඹුරු කෙවුල්-බකමුණා
   54 cm. Dark brown. Upperparts heavily streaked and barred.
   Yellow irides. Small ear-tufts. Tarsi unfeathered.

2. **INDIAN SCOPS-OWL** (176)   *Otus bakkamoena*
   S: Kan-diga Bassa කන්-දිග බස්සා
   23 cm. Irides brown. Dull buff-brown or greyish-brown plumage.
   Underparts with fine wavy bars of reddish brown.

3. **SRI LANKA CHESTNUT-BACKED OWLET** (181)
                                                    Glaucidium castanonotus*
   S: Lanka pitathambala Wana-bassa ලංකා පිටතඹල වන-බස්සා
   20 cm. Reddish brown upperparts, distinctly barred with brown.

4. **ORIENTAL SCOPS-OWL** (175)   *Otus sunia**
   S: Singithi Bassa සිඟිති බස්සා
   19 cm. Greyish brown (sometimes reddish-brown).
   Yellow irides. Small ear-tufts.

5. **SPOT BELLIED EAGLE-OWL** (177)   *Bubo nipalensis*
   S: Ulama උලමා
   61 cm. Dark brown with buff scallop marks.
   Large black and white ear-tufts.

6. **FROGMOUTH** (184) ♂   *Batrachostomus monilieger*
   S: Madi-muhuna මැඩි-මුහුණා
   23 cm. Characteristic bill shape. Yellow irides.
   Male: mottled grey, black and white.

7. **COMMON NIGHTJAR** (187)   *Caprimulgus asiaticus*
   S: Podu bimbassa පොදු බිම්බස්සා
   23 cm. Sandy brown. Small white patch on either side of throat.
   Black streaks on back.

Plate 18

1. **BLACK-BACKED KINGFISHER** (197)   *Cexy erithacus*
   S: Ran-pilihuduwa රන්-පිළිහුඩුවා
   13 cm. Distinctive iridescent plumage.

2. **STORK-BILLED KINGFISHER** (198)   *Pelargopsis capensis*
   S: Manathudu Maha-pilihuduwa මානාතුඩු මහා-පිළිහුඩුවා
   38 cm. Large red bill.

3. **BLACK-CAPPED KINGFISHER** (200)   *Halcyon pileata*
   S: Hisa kalu Dam-pilihuduwa හිස කළු දම්-පිළිහුඩුවා
   30 cm. Black head. White collar on hindneck.

4. **WHITE-THROATED KINGFISHER** (199)   *Halcyon smyrnensis*
   S: Laya sudu Pilihuduwa ළය සුදු පිළිහුඩුවා
   30 cm. White breast and blue upperparts.

5. **COMMON KINGFISHER** (195)   *Alcedo atthis*
   S: Podu mal-pilihuduwa පොදු මල්-පිළිහුඩුවා
   18 cm. Reddish-brown ear coverts.

6. **BLUE-EARED KINGFISHER** (196)   *Alcedo meninting*
   S: Nila karni Mal-pilihuduwa නිල තරණී මල්-පිළිහුඩුවා
   15 cm. Blue ear-coverts.

7. **PIED KINGFISHER** (201) ♂   *Ceryle rudis*
   S: Gomara Kalapu-pilihuduwa ගෝමර කලපු-පිළිහුඩුවා
   30 cm. Frequently hovers.

8 **GREATER PAINTED-SNIPE** (120)
   a:♂ b:♀   *Rostratula benghalensis*
   S: Ulu-kaswatuwa උළු-තැස්වටුවා
   25 cm. Long, slender, straight, bill. Slightly down-curved at tip.
   Female: metallic green above (more colorful during breeding).
   Male and non-breeding female: Browner above.

66

Plate 19

1. **RED-BACKED WOOKPECKER** (219b)
   a:♂ c:♀   *Dinopium benghalense psarodes*
   S: Pita rathu Rath-kerala   පිට රතු රත්-කෑරලා
   28 cm. Back red **Female**: forehead black with white spots.

   BLACK-RUMPED FLAMEBACK (219a)
   b:♂ c:♀   *Dinopium benghalense jaffnense*
   S: Pita ran Rath-kerala   පිට රන් රත්-කෑරලා
   28 cm. Back golden yellow.
   Female: forehead black with white spots.

2. **GREATER FLAMEBACK** (220)
   a:♂ b:♀   *Chrysocolaptes lucidus*
   S: Pita levan Maha-kerala   පිට ලේවන් මහ-කෑරලා
   33 cm. Back deep red (crimson). Black "island formation" on cheek.

3. **STREAK THROATED WOODPECKER** (218)
   a:♂ b:♀   *Picus xanthopygaeus**
   S: Korala udara Kola-kerala   කොරල උදර කොළ-කෑරලා
   29 cm. Bright yellow rump.
   Female: completely black crest.

4. **LESSER YELLOWNAPE** (217) a:♂ b:♀   *Picus chlorolophus*
   S: Peetha pitakara Kola-kerala   පිත පිටකර කොළ-කෑරලා
   20 cm. Yellow Nape. **Male**: red moustachial patch.

5. **YELLOW-CROWNED WOODPECKER** (215)
   a:♂ b:♀   *Dendrocopos mahrattensis*
   S: Pithagra Gomara-kerala   පිතාග්‍ර ගෝමර-කෑරලා
   19 cm. Red abdominal patch. Head with a small crest.

6. **BROWN-CAPPED WOODPECKER** (214) ♂   *Dendrocopos nanus*
   S: Kuru Gomara-karala   කුරු ගෝමර-කෑරලා
   13 cm. Black and white plumage. **Male:** red-streak on occipital region.

Plate 20

1. **INDIAN SWIFTLET** (188)   *Collocalia unicolor**
   S: Indiyanu Kadal-thurithaya ඉන්දියානු කඩැල්-තුරිතයා
   13 cm. Slender, blackish brown. Notched tail.

2. **ASIAN PALM-SWIFT** (190)   *Cypsiurus balasiensis**
   S: Thal-thurithaya තල්-තුරිතයා
   13 cm. Completely dark brown. Slender body.
   Narrow tail fork, thin tail.

3. **LITTLE SWIFT** (192)   *Apus affinis*
   S: Katiya sudu Thurithaya කටිය සුදු තුරිතයා
   15 cm. Completely black with white rump.

4. **BROWN-BACKED NEEDLETAIL** (189)   *Hirundapus giganteus**
   S: Katupenda-thurithaya කටුපෙද-තුරිතයා
   23 cm. White flank stripe continuous with white under tail
   coverts. Spiny edge to tail feathers.

5. **ASHY WOOD SWALLOW-SHRIKE** (238)   *Artamus fuscus*
   S: Alu Sabara-lihiniya අළු සබර-ලිහිණියා
   18 cm. Ashy grey. Swallow-like. Bluish bill.

6. **BARN SWALLOW** (226)   *Hirundo rustica*
   S: Wahi-lihiniya වැහි-ලිහිණියා
   15 cm. Bright dark blue above; blackish blue breast band;
   bright reddish-brown forehead and throat. Underparts white
   to dirty white to brownish. Deeply forked tail.

7. **CRESTED TREE-SWIFT** (193) ♂   *Hemiprocne coronata**
   S: Silu Ruk-thurithaya සිළු රුක්-තුරිතයා
   23 cm. Blue-grey above. Crest on forehead and deeply forked tail.
   Male: sides of face reddish-brown.

8. **RED-RUMPED SWALLOW** (228)   *Hirundo daurica*
   S: Rathu kati Wahi-lihiniya රතු කටි වැහි-ලිහිණියා
   18 cm. Upperparts bright dark blue. Rump reddish-brown.
   Underparts range from white to reddish-brown with heavy streaking
   depending on the subspecies.

Plate 21

1. **SCARLET MINIVET** (252) a:♂ b:♀   *Pericrocotus flammeus*
   S: Maha Minivittha මහ මිණිවිත්තා
   20 cm. **Male:** bright yellowish-red and black plumage.
   Female: yellow, grey and black plumage.

2. **SMALL MINIVET** (251) a:♂ b:♀   *Pericrocotus cinnamomeus*
   S: Kuda Minivittha කුඩා මිණිවිත්තා
   16 cm. **Male:** bright yellowish-red breast and belly.
   Female: dusky white throat, tinged with yellow on the breast.

3. **BROWN-HEADED BARBET** (210)   *Megalaima zeylanica*
   S: Polos Kottoruwa පොළොස් කොට්ටෝරුවා
   26 cm. Brown head.

4. **COPPERSMITH BARBET** (213)   *Magalaima haemacephala*
   S: Botuwa rathu Kottoruwa බොටුව රතු කොට්ටෝරුවා
   15 cm. Forehead and large breast patch, red.
   Belly pale yellowish, broadly streaked with green.

5. **CRIMSON-FRONTED BARBET** (212)   *Megalaima rubricapilla*
   S: Oluwa rathu Kottoruwa ඔළුව රතු කොට්ටෝරුවා
   14 cm. Forehead and small breast patch, red. Lighter green below.

6. **SRI LANKA YELLOW-FRONTED BARBET** (211) *Megalaima flavifrons*
   S: Ran nalal kottoruwa රන් නළල් කොට්ටෝරුවා
   22 cm. Forehead golden yellow. Face and throat, blue.

7. **BLUE-WINGED LEAF BIRD** (256) a:♂ b:♀ *Chloropsis cochinchinensis*
   S: Jerdonge Kolarisiya ජර්දාන්ගේ කොළරිසියා
   18 cm. **Male:** yellowish forehead and sides of neck. Black throat.
   Female: throat bluish green.

8. **COMMON IORA** (254) a:♂ b:♀   *Aegithina tiphia*
   S: Iorava අයෝරාවා
   15 cm. White rump. **Male:** dark blue-black upperpats,
   yellow underparts.
   Female: greenish tinged with yellow upperparts.

Plate 22

1. **WHITE-BELLIED DRONGO** (236)   *Dicrurus caerulescens*
   S: Podu Kauda   පොදු කවුඩා
   24 cm. White vent.

2. **CRESTED DRONGO** (237)   *Dicrurus paradiseus lophorhinus*
   S: Kalu silu Kauda   කළු සිළු කවුඩා
   30-35 cm. Crest on forehead. Tail deeply forked and
   long, without racquet.

3. **RACKET-TAILED DRONGO** (237)   *Dicrurus paradiseus ceylonicus*
   S: Pithipenda Kauda   පිතිපෙද කවුඩා
   30-35 cm. Crest on forehead. Tail deeply forked and long outer tail
   feathers with distinct racquet.

4. **INDIAN ROLLER** (205)   *Coracias bengalensis*
   S: Dumbonna   දුම්බොන්නා
   33 cm. Blue and brown plumage. The blue of the wings
   appears brighter and is the most prominent color in flight.

5. **MALABAR PIED HORNBILL** (209) ♀   *Anthracoceros coronatus*
   S: Poro-kandaththa   පොරෝ-කැඳැත්තා
   61 cm. Bill with a prominent casque.
   Female: naked white skin around the eye.

6. **SRI LANKA GREY HORNBILL** (208) ♂   *Ocyceros gingalensis**
   S: Alu Kandaththa   අළු කැඳැත්තා
   59 cm. Grey plumage. Long, heavy, decurved bill. Long tail.

7. **EURASIAN HOOPOE** (207)   *Upupa epops*
   S: Poroluwa   පොරොළුවා
   30 cm. Black, white and pinkish-brown plumage. Crest and long beak.

Plate 23

1. **SRI LANKA WHITE-FACED STARLING** (239)   *Sturnus senex*
   S: Lanka hisa-sudu Sharikava ලංකා හිස සුදු ශාරිකාවා
   21 cm. White forehead, face and throat.
   Bill greyish-green, dull blue at the base.

2. **MALABAR TROGON** (194) a:♂ b:♀   *Harpactes fasciatus*
   S: Lohawannichchiya ලෝහවන්නිච්චියා
   30 cm. **Male**: white necklace separating black breast
   from brilliant red underparts.
   Female: underparts yellowish brown.

3. **SRI LANKA BLUE MAGPIE** (245)   *Urocissa ornata**
   S: Lanka Kahibella ලංකා කැහිබෙල්ලා
   43 cm. Brown and blue plumage. Tail tipped white.

4. **HILL MYNAH** (244)   *Gracula religiosa*
   S: Podu Salalihiniya පොදු සැළලිහිණියා
   25 cm. Yellow bill. Yellow wattles on side of head and nape.

5. **SRI LANKA MYNAH** (243)   *Gracula ptilogenys*
   S: Lanka Salalihiniya ලංකා සැළලිහිණියා
   25 cm. Reddish-yellow bill. A single pair of wattles.

6. **BLACK-HOODED ORIOLE** (233)
   a: adult.; b:Juv.   *Oriolus xanthornus*
   S: Hisa kalu Kahakurulla හිස කළු කහකුරුල්ලා
   25 cm. Yellow and black plumage.

7. **INDIAN PITTA** (222)   *Pitta brachyura*
   S: Avichchiya අවිච්චියා
   19 cm. Facial pattern with brown and green plumage.
   Distinctive stance.

8. **COMMON MYNAH** (242)   *Acridotheres tristis*
   S: Myna මයිනා
   23 cm. Bill, facial skin and legs yellow.

Plate 24

1. **LONG-TAILED SHRIKE** (230)   *Lanius schach*
   S: Rathu kati Sabarittha රතු කටි සබරිත්තා
   25 cm. Greyish upperback with contrasting reddish-brown rump.

2. **LARGE CUCKOO-SHRIKE** (248) a:♂ b:♀   *Coracina macei**
   S: Maha Kovul-saratittha මහ කොවුල්-සැරටිත්තා
   30 cm. Large, grey bird usually associated with the top canopy.

3. **BLACK-HEADED CUCKOO-SHRIKE** (249)
   a:♂ b:♀   *Coracina melanoptera*
   S: Hisa kalu Kovul-saratittha හිස කළු කොවුල්-සැරටිත්තා
   19 cm. **Male**: Black head and grey plumage.
   Female: upperparts grey-brown. Underparts barred.

4. **COMMON WOOD-SHRIKE** (250)   *Tephrodornis pondicerianus*
   S: Wana-saratittha වන-සැරටිත්තා
   14 cm. White eyebrow. Black face mask.

5. **BROWN SHRIKE** (229)   *Lanius cristatus cristatus*
   S: Dumburu Sabarittha දුඹුරු සබරිත්තා
   19 cm. Black face mask. Plumage brown.

6. **PHILIPPINE SHRIKE** (229)   *Lanius cristatus lucionensis*
   S: Philipina Sabarittha පිළිපීන සබරිත්තා
   19 cm. Crown grey. Black face mask.

7 **BAR-WINGED FLYCATCHER-SHRIKE** (253)   *Hemipus pictatus*
   S: Gomara kalu Saratittha ගෝමර කළු සැරටිත්තා
   15 cm. Black and white plumage. Flycatching habit.
   Breeding birds have a pink wash on the breast.

Plate 25

1. **BLACK BULBUL** (263)   *Hypsipetes leucocephalus**
   S: Kalu-kondaya කළු-කොණ්ඩයා
   23 cm. Bill, legs and irides, bright red.

2. **BLACK-CRESTED BULBUL** (258)   *Pycnonotus melanicterus*
   S: Hisa kalu Kondaya හිස කළු කොණ්ඩයා
   19 cm. Black cap. Tail tipped white. **Male:** red irides;
   Female: brown irides.

3. **WHITE-BROWED BULBUL** (261)   *Pycnonotus luteolus*
   S: Bama-sudu Kondaya බැම-සුදු කොණ්ඩයා
   20 cm. Distinct white eyebrow. Irides red.

4. **SRI LANKA YELLOW-EARED BULBUL** (260) *Pycnonotus penicillatus*
   S: Lanka peetha-kan Kondaya ලංකා පීත-කන් කොණ්ඩයා
   20 cm. Yellow feather tuft behind eye. Distinct facial pattern.

5. **YELLOW-BROWED BULBUL** (262)   *Iole indica**
   S: Bama-kaha Galuguduwa බැම-කහ ගලුගුඩුවා
   20 cm. Bright yellow face and underparts.

6. **RED-VENTED BULBUL** (259)   *Pycnonotus cafer*
   S: Kondaya කොණ්ඩයා
   20 cn. Head black, with crest. White rump. Red vent.

7. **LARGE-BILLED LEAF-WARBLER** (295)   *Phylloscopus magnirostris*
   S: Thuda loku Gas-raviya තුඩ ලොකු ගස්-රැවියා
   12 cm. Prominent yellowish eyebrow. Dark streak through eye.
   Dark crown.

8. **YELLOWISH BREASTED WARBLER** (294)   *Phylloscopus nitidus*
   S: Kola Gas-raviya කොළ ගස්-රැවියා
   10 cm. Paler plumage. Wing bar present. Head lighter in color.

Plate 26

1. **YELLOW-BILLED BABBLER** (270) *Turdoides affinis*
   S: Demalichcha දෙමලිච්චා
   23 cm. Bill and feet pale yellow. Pale orbital region.
   Irides bluish. Usually in groups of around 5-8 birds.

2. **ASHY-HEADED LAUGHING-THRUSH** (271) *Garrulax cinereifrons*
   S: Alu-demalichcha අළු-දෙමලිච්චා
   25 cm. Grey head. Black bill and greyish legs.

3. **SRI LANKA ORANGE-BILLED BABBLER** (269) *Turdoides rufescens*
   S: Rathu Demalichcha රතු-දෙමලිච්චා
   25 cm. Bright reddish-yellow bill and legs.

4. **SCIMITAR BABBLER** (265) *Pomatorhinus horsfieldii**
   S: Da-demalichcha දෑ-දෙමලිච්චා
   22 cm. White eyebrow. Long, yellow decurved bill.

5. **YELLOW-EYED BABBLER** (268) *Chrysomma sinensis*
   S: Peethakshi Thana-demalichcha පීතාක්ෂි තණ-දෙමලිච්චා
   18 cm. Short bill. Reddish-yellow around eyes. Long tail.

6. **TAWNY-BELLIED BABBLER** (266) *Dumetia hyperythra*
   S: Gela Sudu Landu-demalichcha ගෙල සුදු ලඳු-දෙමලිච්චා
   13 cm. White or whitish chin and throat.
   Breast tinged with yellow to reddish-yellow.

7. **DARK-FRONTED BABBLER** (267) *Rhopocichla atriceps*
   S: Hisa kalu Panduru-demalichcha හිස කළ පඳුරු-දෙමලිච්චා
   10 cm. Black forehead and around eye.

8. **SRI LANKA BROWN-CAPPED BABBLER** (264)
   Pellorneum fuscocapillum
   S: Lanka Mudun Bora-demalichcha ලංකා මුදුන් බොර-දෙමලිච්චා
   15 cm. Dark brown to blackish cap.

Plate 27

1. **ASIAN BROWN FLYCATCHER** (272) *Muscicapa dauurica**
   S: Dumburu Masimara දුඹුරු මැසිමාරා
   13 cm. Large eyes with white eye ring. Base of lower mandible yellow.

2. **BROWN-BREASTED FLYCATCHER** (273) *Muscicapa muttui*
   S: Laya dumburu Masimara ළය දුඹුරු මැසිමාරා
   14 cm. Dark brown malar streak. Entire lower mandible yellowish.

3. **GREY-HEADED CANARY FLYCATCHER** (278) *Culicicapa ceylonensis*
   S: Hisa alu Masimara හිස අළු මැසිමාරා
   9 cm. Grey head. Small crest.

4. **ASIAN PARADISE FLYCATCHER** (281) *Terpsiphone paradisi*
   S: Rahanmara රහන්මාරා
   40cm. Male (with tail streamer) 20cm Female.
   (a) Indian or white-phase male: all white except head.
   (b) Dark phase male: upperparts and tail streamers brown.
   (c) Female: brown upperparts, short tail.

5. **TICKELL'S BLUE FLYCATCHER** (277) a:♂ b:♀ *Cyornis tickelliae**
   S: Laya thambilivan Nil-masimara ළය තැඹිලිවන් නිල්-මැසිමාරා
   14 cm. **Male:** bright blue forehead. Throat and breast
   reddish-yellow/brown.
   Female: duller with a paler breast.

6. **KASHMIR FLYCATCHER** (274) a:♂ b:♀ *Ficedula subrubra**
   S: Kashmira laya Rathu-masimara කාෂ්මීර ළය රතු-මැසිමාරා
   13 cm. White patches on base of outer tail feathers.
   Male: Throat, breast and upper belly reddish-yellow.
   Female: Throat, breast and upper belly brown.

7. **SRI LANKA DULL-BLUE FLYCATCHER** (275) *Eumyias sordida**
   S: Lanka Andurunil-masimara ලංකා අඳුරුනිල්-මැසිමාරා
   14 cm. Forehead bright blue. Black lores.

8. **BLACK-NAPED MONARCH** (280) ♂ *Hypothymis azurea**
   S: Nil Radamara නිල් රදමාරා
   15 cm. Crest and nape black.

9. **WHITE-BROWED FANTAIL** (279) *Rhipidura aureola*
   S: Sudu Avenpendamara සුදු අවන්පෙදමාරා
   16 cm. White eyebrow, spots on wing.
   Restless dancing while spreading out tail.

Plate 28

1. **COMMON TAILORBIRD** (292) *Orthotomus sutorius*
   S: Battichcha බට්ටිච්චා
   13 cm. Brown head with greenish upperparts. Tail held erect.

2. **ZITTING CISTICOLA** (283) *Cisticola juncidis*
   S: Rekhankitha Avan-raviya රේඛාංත්කිත අවන්-රැවියා
   13 cm. Buff brown with black streaks.

3. **GREY-BREASTED PRINIA** (284) ♂ *Prinia hodgsonii*
   S: Frankalinge Priniya ෆ්‍රෑන්ක්ලින්ගේ ප්‍රිණියා
   12 cm. Breast with a grey band, complete in the male and
   interrupted in the female.

4. **ASHY PRINIA** (286) *Prinia socialis*
   S: Alupaha Priniya අලුපැහැ ප්‍රිණියා
   12 cm. Underparts orange-brown.

5. **JUNGLE PRINIA** (285) *Prinia sylvatica*
   S: Maha Priniya මහ ප්‍රිණියා
   15 cm. Black bill. Flesh-colored legs.

6. **PLAIN PRINIA** (287) *Prinia inornata*
   S: Bama-sudu Priniya බැම-සුදු ප්‍රිණියා
   14 cm. Eyebrow distinct.

7. **SRI LANKA BUSH-WARBLER** (282) a: ♂ *Bradypterus palliseri*
   S: Lanka Rusi-raviya ලංකා රුසි-රැවියා
   14 cm. Black-brown. Throat light buff.
   Male: red irides.

Plate 29

1. **INDIAN BLUE ROBIN** (303) a:♂ b:♀   *Erithacus brunneus*
   S: Indiyanu Neela-sittibichcha ඉන්දියානු නිල-සිට්ටිබිච්චා
   15 cm. **Male:** white eyebrow, black lores and cheecks.
   Female: brown.

2. **SRI LANKA WHISTLING-THRUSH** (297) ♂   *Myiophoneus blighi*
   S: Lanka Arangaya ලංකා අරංගයා
   20 cm. **Male:** bright blue shoulder patch.

3. **SRI LANKA SPOT-WINGED THRUSH** (300)
   a:♂   *Zoothera spiloptera*
   S: Lanka thithpiya Thirasikaya ලංකා තිත්පිය තිරාසිකයා
   21 cm. Two rows of white spots on wing.

4. **SCALY THRUSH** (301)   *Zoothera dauma*
   S: Pethigomara thirasikaya පෙතිගෝමර තිරාසිකයා
   24 cm. Upperparts with black scaly (crescent-shaped) marks.

5. **PIED THRUSH** (298) a:♂ b:♀   *Zoothera wardii*
   S: Gomara Thirasikaya ගෝමර තිරාසිකයා
   23 cm. **Male:** black and white plumage; white eyebrow.
   Female: whitish with brown spots and scaly
   (crescent-shaped) marks, on breast.

6. **BLACK BIRD** (302)   *Turdus merula*
   S: Kalu-thirasikaya කළු-තිරාසිකයා
   25 cm. Orange bill, eye-ring and legs.
   Female: paler .

Plate 30

1. **PIED BUSH CHAT** (307) a:♂ b:♀ *Saxicola caprata*
   S: Gomara Sittibichcha ගෝමර සිට්ටිබිච්චා
   14 cm. **Male:** white wing patches.
   Female: mottled brown.

2. **WHITE-RUMPED SHAMA** (305)
   a:♂ b:♀ *Copsychus malabaricus*
   S: Vana Polkichcha වන පොල්කිච්චා
   25 cm. White rump; reddish-brown underparts; long tail.

3. **ORIENTAL MAGPIE-ROBIN** (304) a:♂ b:♀ *Copsychus saularis*
   S: Polkichcha පොල්කිච්චා
   20 cm. Black and white plumage.
   Female: duller and greyer.

4. **INDIAN ROBIN** (306) a:♂ b:♀ *Saxicoloides fulicata*
   S: Kalukichcha කළුකිච්චා
   16 cm. **Male:** glossy blue-black, white wing patch visible in flight.
   Female: brownish, with no white wing patch.

5. **GREY WAGTAIL** (314) NBr. *Motacilla cinerea*
   S: Alu Halapenda අළු හැලපෙන්දා
   18 cm. White eyebrow.

6. **RICHARD'S PIPIT** (315) *Anthus richardi**
   S: Richardge Varatichcha රිචර්ඩ්ගේ වැරටිච්චා
   16 cm. Erect stance. Streaked plumage.

7. **RUFOUS-WINGED LARK** (223) *Mirafra assamica*
   S: Akul Thulikava අකුල් තුළිකාවා
   15 cm. Brown, streaked plumage. Crouching stance.

8. **FOREST WAGTAIL** (310) *Dendronanthus indicus**
   S: Kala Halapenda තැලෑ හැලපෙන්දා
   16 cm. Brown breast bands. Tail-wagging habit.

Plate 31

1. **PURPLE SUNBIRD** (321) a:♂ b:♀   *Nectarinia asiatica*
   S: Dam Sutikka   දම් සුටික්කා
   10 cm. Decurved, medium-length bill.
   Male: iridescent plumage.
   Female: greenish (olive)-brown above, whitish eyebrow.

2. **PURPLE-RUMPED SUNBIRD** (320)
   a:♂ b:♀   *Nectarinia zeylonica*
   S: Dam kati Sutikka   දම් කටි සුටික්කා
   10 cm. Short, decurved bill. **Male:** iridescent plumage.
   Female: upperparts greyish brown, underparts dull yellow.

3. **LONG-BILLED SUNBIRD** (322) a:♂ b:♀   *Nectarinia lotenia*
   S: Lotenge Sutikka   ලොටන්ගේ සුටික්කා
   13 cm (including bill). Bill long and decurved.
   Male: iridescent plumage.
   Female: dull olive (brownish yellow) upperparts;
   underparts dull yellow.

4. **SRI LANKA WHITE-THROATED FLOWER PECKER** (318)
   a:♂ b:♀   *Dicaeum vincens*
   S: Lanka Pilalichcha   ලංකා පිළිලිච්චා
   9 cm. **Male:** with white throat patch.
   Female: greyer upperparts.

5. **THICK-BILLED FLOWERPECKER** (317)   *Dicaeum agile*
   S: Thuda mahatha Pilalichcha   තුඩ මහත පිළිලිච්චා
   9 cm. Short bill. Eyes orange-red.

6. **SRI LANKA WHITE-EYE** (323)   *Zosterops ceylonensis*
   S: Lanka Sithasiya   ලංකා සිතාසියා
   10 cm. Darker plumage than oriental white eye.
   White eye ring with a large gap in the anterior region.

7. **ORIENTAL WHITE-EYE** (324)   *Zosterops palpebrosa*
   S: Kuda Sithasiya   කුඩා සිතාසියා
   10 cm. White eye ring with a small gap in the anterior region.

8. **PALE-BILLED FLOWERPECKER** (319)   *Dicaeum erythrorhynchos*
   S: Kuda Pilalichcha   කුඩා පිළිලිච්චා
   8 cm. Slightly curved, pointed, flesh-colored bill.

Plate 32

1. **VELVET-FRONTED BLUE NUTHATCH** (309)   *Sitta frontalis*
   S: Viluda alika Yatikirittha විල්ලුද අළික යටිකිරිත්තා
   13 cm. Forehead black. Pinkish buff belly and flanks. Bright red bill.

2. **GREAT TIT** (308)   *Parus major*
   S: Alu Tikirittha අළු ටිකිරිත්තා
   13 cm. Black, grey and white plumage. Sparrow-like.

3. **STREAKED WEAVER** (326)
   a:♂ -Br.; b:♀/ ♂-NBr.   *Ploceus manyar*
   S: Pan Wadu-kurulla පත් වඩු-කුරුල්ලා
   15 cm. Breast streaked with dark brown.
   Breeding male: bright yellow crown.
   Female; and non-breeding male: plumage brown.

4. **BAYA WEAVER** (327) a:♂ -Br.; b:♀/♂-NBr.   *Ploceus philippinus*
   S: Ruk Wadu-kurulla රුක් වඩු-කුරුල්ලා
   15 cm. **Breeding male:** yellow crown.
   Female and non-breeding male: Crown and back, brown with
   darker brown streaks.

5. **SCALY-BREASTED MUNIA** (331)
   a: adult; b: Juv.   *Lonchura punctulata*
   S: Thith Wee-kurulla තිත් වී-කුරුල්ලා
   10 cm. Brown plumage with lower breast and upper abdomen
   spotted black and white.

6. **WHITE-RUMPED MUNIA** (329) a:adult b:Juv.   *Lonchura striata*
   S: Pita sudu Wee-kurulla පිට සුදු වී-කුරුල්ලා
   10 cm. Rump, lower breast and belly white.

7. **WHITE-THROATED SILVER-BILL** (328)   *Lonchura malabarica*
   S: Gela sudu Wee-kurulla ගෙල සුදු වී-කුරුල්ලා
   10 cm. Sandy brown above. White rump. Long, pointed tail.

8. **BLACK-THROATED MUNIA** (330)   *Lonchura kelaarti*
   S: Kandukara Wee-kurulla කඳුකර වී-කුරුල්ලා
   10 cm. Forehead, face, throat and upper breast, blackish-brown.

9. **HOUSE SPARROW** (325) a:♂ b:♀   *Passer domesticus*
   S: Ge-kurulla / Chatakaya ගේ-කුරුල්ලා/චටකයා
   15 cm. **Male:** black around eyes and on chin and throat.
   Female: sandy brown. Underparts ashy white.

10. **BLACK-HEADED MUNIA** (332)   *Lonchura malacca*
    S: Hisa kalu Wee-kurulla හිස කළු වී-කුරුල්ලා
    10 cm. Contrasting "flat" tricolored plumage. Blue-grey bill.

DESCRIPTIVE TEXT

PODICIPEDIDAE

1. **LITTLE GREBE** Plate 1.6   *Tachybaptus ruficollis**
   Heen Gembithuruwa   හීන් ගෙඹිතුරුවා

   25 cm.
   Fresh or slightly saline stagnant water usually with weeds.
   Common. BrR. LC. Rare in HC.

PELECANIDAE

2. **SPOT-BILLED PELICAN** (Grey Pelican) Plate 1.1 *Pelecanus philippensis*
   Alu Pasthuduwa   අළු පැස්තුඩුවා

   140 cm.
   When swimming ¾ of the body above the water mark.
   Feeds by jabbing bill into the water.
   In flight: slow beat, often glides and soars. Wingspan
   longer than body. Tanks, lagoons. Very common.
   BrR. LCDZ, (birds seen around Colombo are those
   released from the zoo, that have established a breeding
   colony).

PHALACROCORACIDAE

3. **LITTLE CORMORANT** Plate 1.2   *Phalacrocorax niger*
   Punchi Diyakava   පුංචි දියකාවා

   51 cm.
   Tanks, rivers with stagnant pools, lagoons.
   Very common. BrR. LC, occasionally in the HC.

4. **INDIAN CORMORANT** (Indian Shag) Plate 1.4
   Hadapalu Diyakava   හැඩපලු දියකාවා   *Phalacrocorax fuscicollis*

   65 cm.
   Tanks, rivers with stagnant pools, lagoons.
   Very common. BrR. LC.

5. **GREAT CORMORANT** Plate 1.3   *Phalacrocorax carbo*
    Maha Diyakava මහ දියකාවා

    91 cm.
    In flight: neck held slightly above horizontal.
    NBr: nape, hind neck and flanks black.
    Juvenile: browner and with more white on the undersurface.
    Large tanks of DZ.
    Rare. BrR. LCDZ, (the few birds around Colombo are those released
    from the zoo). Large concentrations at Senanayake Samudra.

6. **ORIENTAL DARTER** Plate 1.5   *Anhinga melanogaster*
    Ahikava අහිකාවා

    90 cm.
    Br: more white on neck.
    Tanks, rivers with stagnant pools, lagoons.
    Common. BrR. LC.

ARDEIDAE

7. **LITTLE EGRET** Plate 2.2   *Egretta garzetta*
    Kuda Ali-koka කුඩා ඇලි-කොකා

    61 cm.
    An active feeder, chasing after insects and fishes.
    Marshes, paddy fields, tank edges, mangroves, lagoons.
    Very common. BrR. LC and foot hills along major rivers.

8. **WESTERN REEF EGRET**   *Egretta gularis*
    Mudupara Ali-koka මුහුදුපර ඇලි-කොකා

    59 cm.
    Yellow bill. Greenish legs.
    Two colour phases.
    Slaty black with white stripe on throat and all
    white, sometimes with dark streaks.
    Br: head breast and back plumes present.
    Coastal, lagoons, estuaries.
    Very rare. BrR. LC, along the western and northern coast.

9. **GREY HERON** Plate 2.5   *Ardea cinerea*
    Alu Koka අළු කොකා

    94 cm.
    Marshes, tanks, rivers, mangroves, paddy fields, lagoons.
    Common. BrR. LC.

10. **PURPLE HERON** Plate 2.6   *Ardea purpurea*
    Karaval Koka තරවැල් කොකා

    79 cm.
    Marshes, tanks, mangroves, paddy fields, lagoons.
    Common. BrR. LC.

11. **GREAT EGRET** Plate 2.3   *Casmerodius albus**
    Maha Sudu-koka මහ සුදු-කොකා

    94 cm.
    NBr: dark brown to black legs. Yellow bill and pale green-yellow lores.
    Br: black bill. green lores.
    Marshes, paddy fields, mangroves, tanks, rivers, lagoons.
    Common. BrR. LC.

12. **INTERMEDIATE EGRET** Plate 2.1   *Mesophoyx intermedia**
    Sudu Madi-koka සුදු මැදි-කොකා

    71 cm.
    NBr: dark green to black legs. Pale yellow lores.
    Br: black legs. yellow bill, green lores.
    Marshes, paddy fields, tanks, mangroves, rivers, lagoons.
    Very common. BrR. LC.

13. **CATTLE EGRET** Plate 2.4   *Bubulcus ibis*
    Gava-koka ගව-කොකා

    51 cm.
    NBr: completely white.
    Paddy fields, pasture, marshes.
    Very common. BrR. LC and foot hills up to 800m.

14. **INDIAN POND HERON** Plate 3.1   *Ardeola grayii*
    Kana-koka කණ-කොකා

    46cm.
    Juvenile: brown, heavily streaked.
    Marshes, paddyfields, mangroves, lagoons, tanks, ponds.
    Very common. BrR. All zones.

15. **STRIATED HERON** (Little Green Heron) Plate 2.7
    Kuda pala Kana-koka කුඩා පලා කණ-කොකා   *Butorides striatus*

    52 cm.
    Commonly found skulking among the roots and bases
    of vegetation and on the stilts of "Ja-kotu".
    Juveniles: browner and heavily streaked.
    Along shady rivers and streams, mangroves.
    Common. BrR. LC (common in the coastal belt).

16. **BLACK-CROWNED NIGHT-HERON** Plate 3.2   *Nycticorax nycticorax*
Ra-koka රෑ-කොකා

56 cm.
Roosts during day in colonies. Feeds during the night.
A characteristic 'quack' call heard on take off from roost and
during flight.
Br: reddish legs.
Marshes, mangroves, lagoons.
Common. BrR. LC.

17. **MALAYAN NIGHT-HERON** (Malay Bittern)
Malayanu Thamba-koka මලයානු තඹ-කොකා   *Gorsachius melanolophus*

48 cm.
Brownish-red body with black crown.
Primaries black with white tips. Short, stout,
black bill. An elusive, usually nocturnal bird.
Escapes detection by freezing with head and bill
held upwards.
Marshes, dense swampy forest, reeds, bamboo
thickets, mangroves, gardens with thick cover.
Rare. Migrant. All zones.

18. **YELLOW BITTERN** Plate 3.5   *Ixobrychus sinensis*
Kaha Mati-koka කහ මැටි-කොකා

38 cm, Slim.
In flight: buff wing coverts and black primaries.
Female: reddish-brown crown and streaked underparts.
Juvenile: heavily streaked underparts.
Habits similar to Cinnamon Bittern.
Reed beds, marshes with tall grass, paddy fields, canal beds.
Common. BrR. LCWZ and parts of the DZ.
N.b. The common English name Chinese Little Bittern
adopted by Sibley and Monroe (1990) has not been used.

19. **CINNAMON BITTERN** (Chestnut Bittern) Plate 3.4
Ixobrychus cinnamomeus
Rathu-dumburu Mati-koka රතු-දුඹුරු මැටි-කොකා

38 cm. Slim.
Female: speckled with white on back and wing-coverts.
Juvenile: browner upperparts heavily barred.
Active during early and late hours of the day. Remains
stationary for sometime before making the next move.
Marshes, reed beds, high grass, paddy fields, canal beds,
mangroves. Rare. BrR. LC and foothills.

20. **BLACK BITTERN** Plate 3.3   *Ixobrychus flavicollis**
Kalu Mati-koka කළු මැටි-කොකා

58 cm, Slim.
Active mostly at dusk and dawn. Confined to dark
vegetation during daytime. Marshes, rivers, streams,
reed beds, paddy fields.
Rare. BrR. LC, occasionally foothills.

CICONIIDAE

21. **PAINTED STORK** Plate 4.3   *Mycteria leucocephala**
Lathuvakiya ලතුවැකියා

102 cm.
NBr: paler plumage.
Juvenile: blackish grey or brown plumage.
Feeds in groups. When feeding, the beak is dipped into
the water while moving steadily forward. Legs sometimes
used to churn up mud. Breeds in colonies. Shows elaborate
courtship behaviour such as beak rattling.
Marshes, tanks, paddy fields, lagoons. Common. BrR. LCDZ,
(those around Colombo are birds released from the zoo).

22. **ASIAN OPENBILL** Plate 4.7   *Anastomus oscitans*
Vivara-thuduwa විවර-තුඩුවා

81 cm.
NBr: pale smoky grey and black plumage.
Juvenile: darker.
Marshes, tanks, rivers, paddy fields, lagoons.
Common. BrR. LC.

23. **WOOLY-NECKED STORK** (White-necked Stork) Plate 4.1
Padili Manawa පාදිලි මානාවා   *Ciconia episcopus*

91 cm.
Marshes, rivers, tanks, open grasslands close to water.
Rare. BrR. LCDZ.

24. **BLACK-NECKED STORK** Plate 5.3   *Ephippiorhynchus asiaticus**
Ali-manawa අලි-මානාවා

132 cm. Largest stork in Sri Lanka.
Marshes, rivers, lakes, lagoons. Very rare. BrR. LCDZ
confined presently to the south eastern coast (a few records
of sightings at Annaivilundawa near Battulu Oya on the west coast).

25. **LESSER ADJUTANT**   Plate 5.1   *Leptoptilos javanicus*
Bahuru- manawa   බහුරු-මානාවා

115 cm.
Marshes, drying pools and tanks.
Rare. BrR. LCDZ.

THRESKIORNITHIDAE

26. **GLOSSY IBIS**   Plate 4.5   *Plegadis falcinellus*
Silutu Da-thuduwa   සිලුටු දෑ-තුඩුවා

68 cm.
Br: head and neck area glossy without spots.
Marshes, paddy fields, lagoons.
Rare. Migrant. Restricted locations in the LCDZ
(Kalametiya, Anaivilundawa), and WZ (Bellanvilla - Attidiya).

27. **BLACK-HEADED IBIS** (Oriental Ibis)   Plate 4.4
Sudu Da-kokka   සුදු දෑ-කොකා   *Threskiornis melanocephalus*

76 cm.
Br: red patch on naked skin along inner edge of underwing brighter.
NBr: no back and breast plumes.
Marshes, tank fringes, paddy fields, lagoons.
Very common. BrR. LC. Small numbers in WZ.

28. **EURASIAN SPOONBILL**   Plate 4.2   *Platalea leuco*
Handi Alawa   හැඳි ආලාවා

84 cm.
Marshes, tanks, lagoons.
Rare. BrR. LCDZ.

PHOENICOPTERIDAE

29. **GREATER FLAMINGO**   Plate 5.2   *Phoenicopterus ruber**
Seeyakkaraya   සීයක්කාරයා

127 cm.
White plumage with a tinge of pink and scarlet.
Black primaries and outer secondaries.
Upper and under wing coverts rose pink to bright scarlet.
Long, pinkish -red legs.
Highly saline lagoons.
Common. Migrant. Restricted locations in the LCDZ.

ANATIDAE

30. **FULVOUS WHISTLING DUCK** (Large Whistling Teal)
Maha Thumba-seruwa   මහ තුඹ-සේරුවා   *Dendrocygna bicolor*

50 cm.
Similar to Lesser Whistling Duck, but more
brownish-red. Cap on head extends down the
nape. Side of neck and front pale (buffish). Rump,
upper tail coverts and under-tail coverts whitish.
Cream flank stripes.
Marshes, tanks, mangroves, paddy fields.
Very rare. Migrant. LC.

31. **LESSER WHISTLING DUCK** (Lesser Whistling Teal)   Plate 5.4
Kuda Thumba-seruwa   කුඩා තුඹ-සේරුවා   *Dendrocygna javanica*

40 cm.
In flight: brownish-red upper wing coverts and upper tail coverts, black
flight feathers. Considered a pest to paddy cultivation.
Marshes, tanks, mangroves, paddy fields.
Very common. BrR. LC.

32. **RUDDY SHELDUCK**   *Tadorna ferruginea*
Chakravakaya   චක්‍රවාකයා

64 cm.
Orange-brown plumage with buffy head.
In flight : white wing coverts. Black flight
feathers, green speculum.
Male: narrow black ring round neck.
Tanks, lagoons, rivers.
Very rare. Migrant. LCDZ.

33. **COTTON PYGMY-GOOSE** (Cotton Teal)   Plate 5.7
Mal-sera   මල්-සේරා   *Nettapus coromandelianus*

33 cm.
In flight: male-dark wings with broad white band across
primaries and trailing edge of secondaries.
Female: dark wings with white on trailing edge of secondaries.
Marshes, paddy fields, rivers, lakes.
Common. BrR. LC.

34. **EURASIAN WIGEON** (European Wigeon) *Anas penelope*
Wijaniya Seruwa විජනීය සේරුවා

48 cm.
Male: greyish plumage.
Dark slender neck and upper breast.
White belly. Reddish-brown head with
buffy crown. Short blue-grey feet.
Female: pale, greyish upper wing coverts, dark flight feathers.
Marshes, tanks, lagoons.
Very rare. Migrant. LCDZ.

35. **SPOT-BILLED DUCK** *Anas poecilorhyncha*
Thith-hota Seruwa තිත්-හොට සේරුවා

60 cm.
Blackish plumage. Pale head and neck.
Blackish cap. Feet red. Dark eyeline and
moustachial streak. Bill black with yellow
tip and red spot at base.
Female: mottled dark brown with paler head and neck.
Dark line through eye.
Marshes, rivers, tanks, lagoons.
Very rare. Migrant. LCDZ.

36. **NORTHERN SHOVELER** *Anas clypeata*
Shovale Seruwa ශවල සේරුවා

50 cm.
Very long, broad spatulate bill.
Reddish-brown flanks.
Male: dark green head. White breast.
Reddish-brown belly.
Female: mottled brown. Dark eye stripe. Whitish tail.
In flight: male- pale blue upper wing coverts. Dark flight feathers.
Female-bluish-grey upper wing coverts. Dark flight feathers.
Marshes, tanks, lagoons.
Rare. Migrant. LC.

37. **NORTHERN PINTAIL** Plate 5.5 *Anas acuta*
Ul-penda Seruwa උල්-පෙද සේරුවා

75 cm (male), 53 cm (female).
NBr: male similar to female but, bill black with blue-grey sides.
In flight: green speculum with buff bar in front and white bar behind.
Marshes, tanks, lagoons. Sea-coast.
Very common. Migrant. LC.

38. **GARGANEY** Plate 5.6 *Anas querquedula*
Gargeni Seruwa ගාගනී සේරුවා

38 cm.
Female and NBr male: brown plumage with white patch at base of bill.
In flight: male with pale grey upper wing coverts, dark flight feathers and glossy green speculum.
Female: dark grey upper wing coverts and unglossed blackish speculum.
Marshes, tanks, lagoons, coastal waters.
Very common. Migrant. LC.

39. **COMMON TEAL** (Green-winged Teal) *Anas crecca*
Europiya Seruwa යුරෝපිය සේරුවා

37 cm.
Male: mostly grey plumage, dark reddish-brown head, dark green patch around eye to nape. Long white stripe on scapulars.
Female: mottled brown above.
White belly. Green speculum.
In flight: dark grey upper wing coverts.
Dark wings. Dark head. Green speculum ,white trailing edge.
Marshes, lagoons, tanks.
Very rare. Migrant. LC.

FAMILY ACCIPITRIDAE

40. **OSPREY** *Pandion haliaetus*
Uthuru Kuralaya උතුරු කුරලයා

51-59 cm.
Blackish brown upperparts.
White head and underparts.
Distinct black band through eye to nape.
In flight: dark breast band. Dark flight feathers with black patch at carpal joint.
Sea coast, tanks, rivers, irrigation canals.
Very rare. Migrant. LCDZ.

41. **JERDON'S BAZA** (Brown Baza) *Aviceda jerdoni*
Dumburu Saratukussa දුඹුරු සරටුකුස්සා

45 cm.
Upperparts brown. Reddish-brown barring on lower breast and belly. Long crest often held vertically. Crest feathers tipped broadly with white.
In flight: broad close black banding on primaries.
Forest, forest edge.
Rare. BrR. HC.

42. **BLACK BAZA** *Aviceda leuphotes*
Kalu Saratukussa කළු සරටුකුස්සා

33 cm.
Black plumage with black crest. White breast
band and wing patch. Purplish-brown and buff
bands on belly.
In flight : wings broad and rounded.
Pale grey primaries. Black wing lining.
Open forests, secondary vegetation, villages.
Very rare. Migrant.

43. **ORIENTAL HONEY-BUZZARD** Plate 6.4 *Pernis ptilorhynchus*
Siluvathi Bambarukussa සිළුවැති බඹරුකුස්සා

68 cm.
Plumage highly variable. Upperparts brown to blackish.
Head black to white. Crest usually small, tipped with white.
Underparts almost white to dark brown, streaked or barred.
In flight: small head, long neck. Flight feathers generally white with
black bands in dark birds. The base of primaries has a large white patch.
Open areas close to forests. forest.
Two subspecies present in Sri Lanka.

Pernis ptilorhynchus ruficollis (**Indian Honey-Buzzard**):
Black subterminal and median bands on tail
nearly as wide as paler bands.
Rare. BrR. Distribution uncertain.
Pernis ptilorhynchus orientalis (**Siberian Honey-Buzzard**):
Dark bands on tail narrower than paler bands.
Very rare. Migrant. LCDZ. Single record, near Mannar in 1943
(Phillips, 1978: 14-15).

44. **BLACK-WINGED KITE** Plate 6.2 *Elanus caeruleus*
Pathanukussa පතනුකුස්සා

33 cm.
Open country, grasslands, paddy fields.
Common. BrR. All zones.

45. **BLACK KITE** (Pariah Kite) *Milvus migrans*
Kalu Parakussa කළු පරකුස්සා

61 cm.
Adult with forked tail, (fork disappears when
tail is fanned broadly). General plumage dark
brown to blackish.
In flight: wings angled. Pale wing patch at base of
primaries. Pale head. **Juvenile:** head and underparts streaked with buff. Open and coastal areas,
cities. Very common. BrR. LCDZ northern region.

46. **BRAHMINY KITE** Plate 7.2   *Haliastur indus*
Bamunu Piyakussa බමුණු පියාකුස්සා

45 cm.
Open country near tanks, coast.
Very common. BrR. LC.

47. **WHITE-BELLIED FISH-EAGLE** (White-bellied Sea-Eagle) Plate 7.4
Sethodara Diyakussa සේතොන්දර දියකුස්සා   *Haliaeetus leucogaster*

71 cm.
Sea coast, large tanks, lagoons.
Common. BrR. LCDZ and mid-country.

48. **GREY-HEADED FISH-EAGLE** Plate 7.3   *Ichthyophaga ichthyaetus*
Waw Masukussa වැව් මසුකුස්සා

70 cm.
Forested waterways, tanks.
Rare. BrR. LCDZ.

49. **CRESTED SERPENT-EAGLE** Plate 6.3   *Spilornis cheela*
Sarapukussa සරපුකුස්සා

51-71 cm.
Forest.
Very common. BrR. All zones.

50. **WESTERN MARSH HARRIER** Plate 7.6   *Circus aeruginosus*
Waguru Harikussa වගුරු හැරිකුස්සා

48 - 56 cm.
Adult Male: head buff with lores
and around the eye black.
Back, scapulars and median coverts dark brown.
Upper tail coverts grey or mixed grey and brown.
Tail silver grey. Upper breast to undertail coverts
brownish-red to dark brown with darker streaks.
In flight: under side of wings grey and outer primaries black.
Female and juvenile: pale patch at base of primaries.
Barred tail.
Marshes, open country. Common. Migrant. All zones.

51. **PALLID HARRIER**   *Circus macrourus*
    Sudumali Harikussa සුදුමැලි හැරිකුස්සා

43 - 48 cm.
Male: upper tail coverts indistinctly barred
grey and white.
In flight: pale grey upperparts.
Female: brown plumage.
N.b.: the females of Pale Harrier and Montagu's
Harrier are indistinguishable in the field and both
are difficult to distinguish from the female Pied Harrier.
Open country, marshes.
Rare. Migrant. All zones.

52. **PIED HARRIER** Plate 7.5   *Circus melanoleucos*
    Kalu-sudu harikussa කළු-සුදු හැරිකුස්සා

43 - 45 cm.
Female: head and upperparts dark brown .
Underparts pale reddish-brown with dark
brown streaks. Whitish rump.
In flight: dusky or blackish bands on flight feathers.
Juvenile: darker than female.
White ruff prominent.
Marshes, open country.
Rare. Migrant. All zones.

53. **MONTAGU'S HARRIER**   (*pygargus*
    Montegu Harikussa මොන්ටේගු හැරිකුස්සා

43 cm.
Adult Male: plumage grey. Grey upper tail
coverts (rump).
Secondaries paler than mantle.
Narrow black bar across base of secondaries.
Outer tail feathers with dark bars.
Belly, thighs and flanks narrowly streaked with red dish-brown.
Female: dark brown upperparts. Small white patch on upper tail
coverts. Underparts dark. Tail has narrow and less distinct pale tip.
In flight: wings and tail long. Wings held in shallow 'V' and angled.
Marshes, open country. Rare. Migrant. All zones.

54. **CRESTED GOSHAWK** *Accipiter trivirgatus*
Siluvathi Kurulugoya සිළුවැති කුරුළුගොයා

40 cm. Wing tips extend to basal half of tail.
Tibial coverts boldly barred with blackish-brown.
Male: upperparts dark brown.
White on tips of upper tail coverts.
Underparts: white. Dark throat stripe.
Streaked breast. Belly barred with reddish-brown.
Head and crest grey.
Female: head browner.
In flight: throat stripe, streaked breast, barred belly distinct.
Juvenile: upperparts brown, underparts white with
reddish-brown streaks.
Forests, secondary vegetation.
Rare. BrR. All zones.

55. **SHIKRA** Plate 6.1 *Accipiter badius*
Kurulugoya කුරුළුගොයා

30 - 35 cm.
Female: larger. Browner upperparts.
Forest, scrub, gardens.
Very common. BrR. All zones.

56. **BESRA** (Besra Sparrowhawk) *Accipiter virgatus*
Besra Kurulugoya බෙස්රා කුරුළුගොයා

30 - 35 cm.
Brown upper plumage.
Broad, dark mesial stripe on white throat.
Underparts closely barred with brown.
Male: upperparts blackish brown to dark slaty
grey with blackish head.
Breast and belly brownish grey to reddish - brown
with broad white and blackish streaks in centre of breast.
Barred belly.
Female: similar to male but more browner and less
reddish-brown on underparts.
In flight : mesial stripe, barred belly and streaked breast.
Juvenile: paler in colour. Tail bands darker.
Forest, gardens.
Rare. BrR. All zones.

57. **COMMON BUZZARD**   *Buteo buteo*
Podu Lassikussa පොදු ලැසිකුස්සා

51 - 56 cm.
Plumage variable. Upperparts dark brown.
Underparts buff to dark brown. Dark belly
bars. Streaked breast.
In flight: Wing held slightly forward and above
body. White patch at base of primaries. Dark
carpal patches, indistinct banding on wing. Dark
belly band and some streaking on breast. Broad
blackish sub terminal band on tail.
Juvenile: similar to adult but has narrow tail bands.
Forest, tank fringes. Rare. Migrant. All zones.

58. **BLACK EAGLE** Plate 6.7   *Ictinaetus malayensis*
Kalukussa කළුකුස්සා

69 cm.
Forest, forest edge.
Rare. BrR. HZ and LCDZ foothills.

59. **BOOTED EAGLE**   *Hieraaetus pennatus*
Kesarupa Rajaliya කෙසරූපා රාජාලියා

48 - 56 cm.
Brown upperparts. Paler (fawn colored) head.
Pale buff areas on wing. Buff-white below with fine
marks on throat and breast. Occurs also as a dark
phase, in which except the tail, the underparts
are chocolate brown.
In flight: tail square, long, unbanded. Buffy body
and wing lining. Pale tail contrasts with dark primaries
and secondaries.
Juvenile: Like adult but paler.
Forest, forest edge. Very rare. Migrant. All zones.

60. **RUFOUS-BELLIED EAGLE** (Rufous-bellied Hawk-eagle)
Rathodara Rajaliya රතෝදර රාජාලියා
                                                  *Hieraaetus kienerii**

51 cm.
Small crest. Upperparts black. Throat and
upper breast white. Lower breast and belly dark
reddish-brown. Tail with bands.
In flight: distinct reddish-brown belly and wing
band. Large round pale patch at base of primaries,
visible above and below.**Juvenile**: upperparts blackish-brown.
Head dark brown. White eyebrow and forehead. Large black patch
around eye. Underparts white, unmarked. Dark patch on upper flanks.
Forests, forest edge. Rare. BrR. All zones.

61. **CHANGEABLE HAWK-EAGLE** (Crested Hawk-eagle)   Plate 6.5
   Kondakussa   කොණ්ඩකුස්සා   *Spizaetus cirrhatus*

   69 cm.
   Color varies considerably.
   Underparts from almost brown to white.
   Upperparts pale to dark brown.
   Forests, open areas with trees, secondary growth.
   Common. BrR. All zones.

62. **MOUNTAIN HAWK-EAGLE**   Plate 6.6   *Spizaetus nipalensis*
   Kandukara Kondakussa   කඳුකර කොණ්ඩකුස්සා

   72 cm (male); 80cm (female).
   Forests.
   Rare. BrR. HC, occassionally LCWZ.

FALCONIDAE

63. **COMMON KESTREL**   Plate 7.1   *Falco tinnunculus*
   Parisarikussa   පරිසාරිකුස්සා

   34 cm.
   Female: upperparts and tail reddish-brown with narrow black bars.
   Open country, forest, scrub.

   Three subspecies,
   seperable only by color intensity.
   Falco tinnunculus tinnunculus (**European Kestrel**).
   Common. Migrant. All zones.
   Falco tinnunculus interstinctus (**Eastern Kestrel**).
   "Dark upperparts, heavily barred".
   "Upperparts paler". Very rare. Migrant. All zones.
   Falco tinnunculus objurgatus (**Indian Kestrel**).
   "More brick-red upperparts".
   Very rare. BrR. HC.

64. **ORIENTAL HOBBY**   *Falco severus*
   Hobby Parisarikussa   හොබි පරිසාරිකුස්සා

   25 cm.
   Upperparts slaty grey. Blackish head.
   Primaries and secondaries unstreaked.
   Deep brownish-red underparts except throat
   which is pale reddish-brown or buff.
   Juvenile: similar to adult but underparts
   streaked with black.
   Forests, cliffs.
   Very rare. Migrant. HC.

65. **PEREGRINE / SHAHEEN FALCON** *Falco peregrinus*
Peradiga/Shahin Parisarikussa පෙරදිග/ශාහීන් පරිසාරිකුස්සා

38-48 cm.
Upperparts slaty grey, barred with black.
Cheeks white with broad black moustache.
Head blackish.
In flight: large wings. Wing
coverts darker than the flight feathers.
Tail indistinctly barred.
Juvenile: head like adult, but
general plumage browner and underparts heavily streaked.
Open country, forest, cliffs and rocks.

Two subspecies.
Falco peregrinus japonensis (**Peregrine falcon**).
Underparts white with narrow black markings except throat and upper breast.
Very rare. Migrant. All zones.
Falco peregrinus peregrinator (**Shaheen falcon**).
Underparts reddish-brown with indistinct black barring.
Rare. BrR. All zones.

PHASIANIDAE

66. **PAINTED FRANCOLIN** (Painted Partridge) *Francolinus pictus*
Thith Vatu-kukula තිත් වටු-කුකුළා

30 cm.
Upperparts brownish, spotted with black,
scalloped and finely barred with white.
Supercilium and face, pale brownish-red.
Underparts black, heavily spotted with white.
Centre of abdomen and vent reddish-brown.
Male: brownish-red throat.
Female: whitish throat.
In flight : white spotted plumage. Black outer tail
feathers and rich reddish-brown underparts. Cambered wing.
Juvenile: like female, with black arrow-shaped marks on the flanks and
lower breast.
Dry patana park land.
Rare. BrR. DZ (foothills and mountains of Uva Province).

67. **GREY FRANCOLIN** (Indian Grey Partridge)
Alu Vatu-kukula අළු වටු-කුකුලා   *Francolinus pondicerianus*

33 cm.
Greyish-brown, reddish-brown and brownish-red
above with buff and black markings.
Underparts pale buff and brownish-red, narrowly
cross barred on foreneck and upper breast.
Finer lines of black on abdomen and flanks.
Prominent yellowish-brown throat patch with a
black margin.
In flight : reddish-brown tail very clear.
Juvenile: paler. Black margin of throat patch almost absent.
Open land, coast, scrub-lands.
Common. BrR. LCDZ - Puttlam to Jaffna peninsula.

68. **RAIN QUAIL** (Black-breasted Qnail)   *Coturnix coromandelica*
Laya kalu Watuwa ලය කළු වටුවා

18 cm.
Pale brown plumage with black and
yellowish buff streaks.
Male: dark jet black marks on face and throat.
Cheeks white. Upper breast black.
Black streaks on under side.
Female: chin and throat creamy buff. Breast spotted with blackish.
Dry scrub, grasslands, cultivations.
Very rare. Migrant. All zones.

69. **BLUE-BREASTED QUAIL**   Plate 8.3   *Coturnix chinensis*
Laya nil Watuwa ලය නිල් වටුවා

15 cm.
Grasslands, scrub.
Common. BrR. All zones.

70. **JUNGLE BUSH-QUAIL**   *Perdicula asiatica*
Panduru-watuwa පඳුරු-වටුවා

15 cm.
Male: upperparts brown, streaked and
mottled with black and buff. Prominent buff
and brownish-red superciliary stripe from
forehead down side of neck. Underparts white,
closely barred with black. Chin and throat bright,
brownish-red.
Female: upperparts like male. Underparts-pale pinkish -reddish-brown,
no barring. Brownish-red throat patch present.
Grasslands, scrub.
Rare. BrR. LCDZ and HC.

71. **SRI LANKA SPURFOWL** Plate 8.5   *Galloperdix bicalcarata*
Lanka Haban-kukula ල·කා හබන්-කුකුළා

33 cm.
Endemic species.
Humid forests.
Rare. BrR. WZ, eastern and southern sector of DZ.

72. **SRI LANKA JUNGLEFOWL** Plate 8.1   *Gallus lafayetii*
Lanka Wali-kukula ල·කා වලි-කුකුළා

70cm (male) 35 cm (female).
Endemic species.
Forests and scrub.
Common. BrR. All zones.

73. **INDIAN PEAFOWL** Plate 8.4   *Pavo cristatus*
Monara/Sebeda මොණරා/සෙබඩ

250 cm (male with train); 102-117 cm (female and male without train).
Open-country, scrubland, chena, grassy borders of tanks.
Common. BrR. LCDZ.

TURNICIDAE

74. **BARRED BUTTON-QUAIL** (Bustard-quail) Plate 8.2
Bola-watuwa බෝල-වටුවා   *Turnix suscitator*

16 cm.
Forest, scrub, grassland, cultivations.
Common. BrR. All zones.

RALLIDAE

75. **SLATY-LEGGED CRAKE** (Banded Crake)   *Rallina eurizonoides*
Pati Keraliya පටි කෙරළියා

25 cm.
Bill grey black. Crown, hind neck and
upper breast brownish-red.
Broad black and white barring on lower breast
and belly. Back brown. Legs grey.
Female: top of crown, back of neck and
top of crown back of neck and back brown.
Face and breast pale.
Swampy jungles, thickets.
Common. Migrant. All zones.

76. **SLATY-BREASTED RAIL** (Blue-breasted Banded Rail)
Laya nil Reluva ළය නිල් රෙලුවා   *Gallirallus striatus**

25 cm.
Longish red bill. Brownish-red crown.
Ashy-blue breast and foreneck.
Rest of plumage barred with white.
Female: duller above and whitish on belly.
Marshes, mangroves, paddy fields.
Rare. BrR. All zones.

77. **WHITE-BREASTED WATERHEN**   Plate 3.6
Laya sudu Korawakka ළය සුදු කොරවක්කා   *Amaurornis phoenicurus*

33 cm.
Twitching upturned tail.
Marshes, mangroves, paddy fields.
Very common. BrR. All zones.

78. **BAILLON'S CRAKE**   *Porzana pusilla*
Miti Vil-keraliya මිටි විල්-කෙරළියා

19 cm.
Short greenish bill. Brown upperparts with
black and white streaks. Underparts grey.
Flanks and under tail coverts barred
(black and white). Brownish streak through
eye over ear-coverts to side of neck.
Marshes.
Very rare. Migrant. LC and mid country.

79. **RUDDY-BREASTED CRAKE**   *Porzana fusca**
Rathu Vil-keraliya රතු විල්-කෙරළියා

22 cm.
Yellow-red legs. Forehead, forecrown, sides
of face, throat and lower breast, brownish-red.
Chin and centre of throat whitish. Under tail
coverts blackish with white bars.
Rest of plumage brownish.
Marshes, reeds.
Rare. BrR. All zones.

80. **WATERCOCK**   *Gallicrex cinerea*
    Kora   කෝරා

    43 cm.
    Male: (breeding) bill yellow.
    Head shield and legs red. Body blackish
    with buffy under tail coverts.
    Female and non breeding male: greenish-yellow
    bill and legs. Buffy brown general plumage, scalloped
    appearence above and narrow dark barring below.
    Paddy fields, marshes, reed beds.
    Rare. BrR. LC.

81. **PURPLE SWAMPHEN** (Purple Coot)   Plate 3.7   *Porphyrio porphyrio*
    Nil Kithala   නිල් තිතලා

    43 cm.
    Marshes with reeds, paddy fields.
    Very common. BrR. LC.

82. **COMMON MOORHEN**   Plate 3.8   *Gallinula chloropus*
    Galinuwa   ගැලිනුවා

    33 cm.
    Marshes, paddy fields.
    Common. BrR. LC. Small numbers in WZ.

83. **COMMON COOT** (Black Coot)   *Fulica atra*
    Kalu Kithala   කළු තිතලා

    38 cm.
    Blackish plumage. Darker neck and head.
    Narrow white trailing edge to secondaries.
    Legs green.
    Marshes, tanks.
    Very rare. BrR. LCDZ.

JACANIDAE

84. **PHEASANT-TAILED JACANA**   Plate 4.8   *Hydrophasianus chirurgus*
    Savulpenda Diyasana   සැවුල්පෙඳ දියසෑනා

    30 cm (breeding male 50 cm).
    Marshes, ponds with reeds and lotus.
    Very common. BrR. LC.

HAEMATOPODIDAE

85. **EURASIAN OYSTERCATCHER**   Plate 11.1
Bolugulla   බොලුගුල්ලා   *Haematopus ostralegus*

45 cm.
Sandy or rocky areas on seashore and estuaries.
Very rare. Migrant. LCDZ - north western coast.

CHARADRIIDAE

86. **PACIFIC GOLDEN PLOVER** (Golden Plover) Plate 9.4   *Pluvialis fulva**
Ran Maha-oleviya   රන් මහ-ඔලෙවියා

25 cm.
Marshes, grassy areas bordering tanks, lagoons.
Very common. Migrant. LC.

87. **GREY PLOVER**   Plate 9.3   *Pluvialis squatarola*
Alu Maha-oleviya   අළු මහ-ඔලෙවියා

28 cm.
Marshes, mud flats, lagoons.
Common. Migrant. LC.

88. **LITTLE RINGED PLOVER**   Plate 9.8   *Charadrius dubius*
Heen mala Oleviya   හීන් මාල ඔලෙවියා

16 cm.
Marshes, mud flats, sand flats, gravel banks, lagoons.

Two subspecies. Indistinguishable in the field.
Charadrius dubius jerdoni **(Jerdon's Little Ringed Plover)**.
"Wing length 102-114 mm"
Common. BrR. LCDZ.
Charadrius dubius curonicus **(Little Ringed Plover).**
"Wing length 115-121 mm".
Common. Migrant. LC.

89. **KENTISH PLOVER**   Plate 9.7   *Charadrius alexandrinus*
Kentiya Oleviya   තෙන්ටිය ඔලෙවියා

18 cm.
Marshes, sand-flats, mud flats, sea coast, lagoons.

Two subspecies indistinguishable in the field.
Charadrius alexandrinus seebohmi **(Ceylon Kentish Plover).**
"Wing length 93-107 mm".
Common. BrR. LCDZ.
Charadrius alexandrinus alexandrinus **(Kentish Plover).**
"Wing length 106-118 mm".
Very common. Migrant. LC.

90. **LESSER SAND PLOVER / MONGOLIAN PLOVER**   Plate 9.6
Kuda vali Oleviya   කුඩා වැලි ඔලෙවියා   *Charadrius mongolus*

20 cm.
Marshes, mud-flats, sand-flats, lagoons.

Two subspecies.
Charadrius mongolus atrifrons **(Lesser Sand Plover).**
NBr. "Obscure sandy brown facial markings tinged yellowish
and pale-buff supercillium."
Common. Migrant. LC.
Charadrius mongolus mongolus **(Mongolian Plover).**
NBr. "Distinct dark-brown and white facial pattern."
Rare. Migrant. LCDZ.

91. **GREATER SAND PLOVER**   Plate 9:5   *Charadrius leschenaultii*
Maha vali Oleviya   මහ වැලි ඔලෙවියා

23 cm.
Legs pale brown or grey.
In flight: toes project beyond tail.
Marshes, mud flats, sand flats, lagoons.
Common. Migrant. LCDZ.

92. **CASPIAN PLOVER**   *Charadrius asiaticus*
Caspiyanu Oleviya   කැස්පියානු ඔලෙවියා

20 cm.
NBr: entire breast grey-brown. Brown band
across eye does not extend to the lores.
Forehead and eyebrows sometimes buff. Bill very
much thinner than that of Large Sand Plover.
In flight : whitish wing lining and white axillaries.
Marshes, mud flats, sand flats, coast, lagoons.
Rare. Migrant. LCDZ.

Br

NBr

118

93. **YELLOW-WATTLED LAPWING**   Plate 10.6   *Vanellus malabaricus*
Kaha karamal Kirala   කහ තරමල් කිරලා

28 cm.
Open dry country with very short grass.
Common. BrR. LCDZ.

94. **RED-WATTLED LAPWING**   Plate 10.5   *Vanellus indicus*
Rath karamal Kirala   රත් තරමල් කිරලා

33 cm. Call - "did-he-do-it".
Open country, dry mud-flats, short grasslands.
Very Common. BrR. LC. Recent records in the HC.

SCOLOPACIDAE

95. **EURASIAN WOODCOCK**   *Scolopax rusticola*
Badi-kukula   බැදි-කුකුළා

35 cm.
Crown barred. No broad, buffy streaks on
upperparts, but mottled shades of rusty brown
and buff. Underparts completely barred with brown
and buff. Usually nocturnal.
In flight : broad wings with rounded tips, owl like flight.
Forest, secondary vegetation.
Very rare. Migrant. HC.

96. **WOOD SNIPE**   *Gallinago nemoricola*
Wana Kas watuwa   වන කැස් වටුවා

30 cm.
Dark brown with diffuse pattern of black,
reddish-brown and buff-streaks.
Dark brown barring on entire underparts.
In flight: flight heavy and slow. Rounded wings.
Bill pointed down.
Marshes with heavy cover, paddy fields.
Very rare. Migrant. HC.

97. **PINTAIL SNIPE**   Plate 10.4   *Gallinago stenura**
Penda ul Kas watuwa   පෙද උල් කැස් වටුවා

25 cm.
In flight : flight slow, heavy, direct (ie. with little zig
zag movement). Marsh areas, paddy fields, drier areas
not frequented by other snipes.
Common. Migrant. All zones.

98. **COMMON SNIPE** *Gallinago gallinago**
Avan penda Kas watuwa අවන් පෙද කැස් වටුවා

28 cm.
Field identification difficult because of similarity
to Pintail Snipe. Upperparts dark brown heavily
streaked with black, brownish-red and buff.
Lower parts whitish. Very long (6 cm) slender
bill. Broad buffy streaks on head.
In flight : narrow but clear white band on trailing
edge of secondaries. Fast highly erratic flight.
Marshes, paddy fields.
Rare. Migrant. WZ and north western DZ.

99. **JACK SNIPE** *Lymnocryptes minimus**
Heen Ka-watuwa හීන් කැ-වටුවා

20 cm.
Absence of pale streak on centre of dark crown.
Pointed wedge shaped, dark brown tail,
without white or reddish-brown.
Metallic green and purple sheen on upper
plumage. Bill short.
In flight : no white or reddish-brown on tail.
Marshes.
Rare. Migrant. LC (mainly western and southern sector).

100. **BLACK-TAILED GODWIT** Plate 11.3 *Limosa limosa*
Penda kalu Gohoduvittha පෙද කළු ගොහොදුවිත්තා

40 cm.
In flight: white wing bar and legs project well beyond tail. Marshes,
coast, mud flats, paddy fields, lagoons.

Two subspecies which are difficult to distinguish in the field.
Limosa limosa limosa **(Black-tailed Godwit).**
Large; wing 200 - 240 mm, culmen 85–126 mm.
Common. Migrant. LCDZ.
Limosa limosa melanuroides **(Eastern Black-tailed Godwit).**
Small; wing 176 - 207 mm, culmen 77–87mm.
Very rare. Migrant. LCDZ.

101. **BAR-TAILED GODWIT** Plate 11.4 *Limosa lapponica*
Iri penda Gohoduvittha ඉරි පෙද ගොහොදුවිත්තා

38 cm.
In flight: toes project slightly beyond tail.
Marshes, coast, mud-flats, lagoons.
Very rare. Migrant. LCDZ.

102. **WHIMBREL** Plate 10.2   *Numenius phaeopus*
Vimburaliya විඹුරළියා

43 cm.
Marshes, coast, mud flats, lagoons.
Migrant. LCDZ.

Two subspecies .
Numenius phaeopus phaeopus **(Common Whimbrel)**.
 "General colour paler; dark bars and streaks on body less heavy"
Common.
Numenius phaeopus variegatus **(Eastern Whimbrel)**.
"General colour darker; dark bars and streaks
broader and more numerous".
Rare.

103. **EURASIAN CURLEW** Plate 10.1   *Numenius arquata*
Kalikaya තාලිතයා

59 cm.
Marshes, sea-coast, mud flats, lagoons.
Migrant. LC.

Two subspecies.
Numenius arquata arquata **(Common Curlew)**.
"Axillaries white with bold blackish streaks".
Rare.
Numenius arquata orientalis **(Eastern Curlew)**.
"Axillaries pure white or thinly streaked with blackish".
Common.

104. **SPOTTED REDSHANK**   *Tringa erythropus*
Thith rathpa Silibilla තිත් රන්පා සිළිබිල්ලා

30 cm.
NBr: greyish-brown and white plumage with
longish orange-red legs. Slender straight black
bill with red base. White supercilium. Brown lores.
Br: black plumage, upperparts spotted with white.
In flight: white rump. Secondaries barred, paler
than rest. Feet trail beyond tail. Distinguished
from common red-shank by absence of a white wing bar.
Marshes, coast, mud flats, lagoons, paddy fields.
Rare. Migrant. LCDZ.

105. **COMMON REDSHANK** Plate 11.6   *Tringa totanus*
Rathpa Silibilla රන්පා සිළිබිල්ලා

28 cm.
In flight: broad white bar on trailing edge of wing.
Marshes, mud flats, coasts, lagoons.
Very common. Migrant. LC.

106. **MARSH SANDPIPER** Plate 12.3   *Tringa stagnatilis*
Waguru Silibilla වගුරු සිලිබිල්ලා

25 cm.
Marshes, mud flats, lagoons.
Very common. Migrant. LC.

107. **COMMON GREENSHANK** Plate 11.5   *Tringa nebularia*
Palapa Silibilla පලාපා සිලිබිල්ලා

35 cm.
In flight: legs project beyond tail.
Marshes, mud flats, coast, lagoons.
Common. Migrant. LC.

108. **GREEN SANDPIPER** Plate 12.1   *Tringa ochropus*
Kola Silibilla කොළ සිලිබිල්ලා

24 cm.
Eyebrow does not extend beyond eye.
Legs blackish green.
In flight: under wing coverts dark, legs do not project much beyond tail.
Distinguished from the Common Sandpiper (111) by the white rump.
Inland marshes, paddy fields, tank and stream banks.
Rare. Migrant. LC.

109. **WOOD SANDPIPER** Plate 12.2   *Tringa glareola*
Wana Silibilla වන සිලිබිල්ලා

23 cm.
Eyebrow extends beyond eye.
Legs greenish yellow.
In flight: under wing coverts white.
Legs project beyond tail.
Marshes, paddy fields, mud flats, lagoons.
Very common. Migrant. All zones.

110. **TEREK SANDPIPER** Plate 12.4   *Tringa cinerea* *
Terek silibilla ටෙරෙක් සිලිබිල්ලා

25 cm.
Marshes, mud flats, lagoons.
Rare. Migrant. LCDZ.

111. **COMMON SANDPIPER** Plate 12.6   *Tringa hypoleucos*
Podu Silibilla පොදු සිලිබිල්ලා

20 cm.
Characteristic flight with shallow flickering of bowed wings.
Marshes, ponds, coast, mud flats, paddy fields, lagoons.
Very common. Migrant. All zones.

112. **RUDDY TURNSTONE** Plate 11.7   *Arenaria interpres*
Galharawanna ගල්හරවන්නා

20 cm.
Marshes, coast, mud flats, lagoons.
Very common. Migrant. LCDZ.

113. **SANDERLING**   *Calidris alba*
Wali Hinna වැලි හින්නා

20 cm.
NBr: very white in appearance, especially
the head. Black patch at bend of closed wing.   Br
Bill and legs black.   NBr
Br: head neck and breast deep reddish brown with
small dark brown streaks contrasting with white underparts.
In flight: broad white wing bar.
Coastal areas, mudflats.
Rare. Migrant. LCDZ.

114. **LITTLE STINT** Plate 12.7   *Calidris minuta*
Heen Hinna හීන් හින්නා

15 cm.
Marshes, mud-flats, lagoons, paddy fields.
Very common. Migrant. LC.

115. **TEMMINCK'S STINT** Plate 12.9   *Calidris temminckii*
Temminck Hinna ටෙමිංක් හින්නා

15 cm.
Marshes, mud-flats, lagoons.
Rare. Migrant. LCDZ.

116. **LONG-TOED STINT** Plate 12.8   *Calidris subminuta*
Padangili diga Hinna පාදැඟිලි දිග හින්නා

17 cm.
In flight: toes project a little beyond tail.
Marshes, paddy fields, mud-flats, lagoons.
Rare. Migrant. LCDZ.

117. **CURLEW SANDPIPER** Plate 12.5   *Calidris ferruginea*
Kalika Hinna කාලිකා හින්නා

21 cm.
Marshes, mud-flats, lagoons.
Very common. Migrant. LC.

118. **BROAD -BILLED SANDPIPER** *Limicola falcinellus*
Palal Thudu-hinna පළල් තුඩු-හින්නා

18 cm.
Long black bill slightly decurved at tip.
Legs blackish. White, split supercilium. Dark mottled
greyish upperparts. Narrow dark streaks
on head, nape and mantle.
NBr: underparts white. Faint dark streaks
on neck. Blackish shoulder patch.
In flight: dark patch along center of tail,
upper tail coverts and rump.
Marshes, mud-flats, lagoons.
Very rare. Migrant. LCDZ.

119. **RUFF**   Plate 11.2 *Philomachus pugnax*
Lovichchiya ලොවිච්චියා

Male. 30 cm, Female 25 cm.
Marshes, mud-flats, lagoons.
Common. Migrant. LCDZ.

ROSTRATULIDAE

120. **GREATER PAINTED-SNIPE**   Plate 18.8 *Rostratula benghalensis*
Ulu-kaswatuwa උළු-කැස්වටුවා

25 cm.
Whitish "spectacles" with white to buff behind eye.
Marshes, paddy fields.
Rare. BrR. All zones.

RECURVIROSTRIDAE

121. **BLACK-WINGED STILT**   Plate 4.6 *Himantopus himantopus*
Piyapath kalu Ipalpava පියාපත් කළු ඉපල්පාවා

38 cm.
Juvenile: brownish back with pale edges to feathers.
Marshes, mud-flats, paddy fields, lagoons.
Very common. BrR. LC.

122. **PIED AVOCET**   Plate 10.3 *Recurvirostra avosetta*
Avasattha අවසැත්තා

43 cm.
Marshes, mud-flats, lagoons.
Rare. Migrant. LCDZ.

DROMADIDAE

123. CRAB PLOVER
Kakulu-oleviya කකුළු-ඔලෙවියා

Dromas ardeola

38 cm.
Black back and primaries, rest of plumage white.
Heavy tern-like black bill.
Grey legs.
In flight: white plumage with black back and
flight feathers.
Sea-coast, sand islands.
Very rare. Probably BrR. DZ (northern region).

BURHINIDAE

124. EURASIAN THICK-KNEE (Stone-Curlew)   Plate 9.1
Kuda Golu-kalikaya කුඩා ගොළු-කාලිකයා   *Burhinus oedicnemus*

40 cm.
Open country, rivers and sand banks.
Common. BrR. LC.

125. GREAT THICK-KNEE (Stone Plover) Plate 9.2
Maha Golu-kalikaya මහ ගොළු-කාලිකයා   *Burhinus recurvirostris**

50 cm.
Rivers, dry open areas close to tanks, lagoons.
Common. BrR. LCDZ.

GLAREOLIDAE

126. INDIAN COURSER
Indiyanu Javasariya ඉන්දියානු ජවසැරියා

Cursorius coromandelicus

26 cm.
Lapwing-like. Sandy brown, reddish-brown and
black underparts. Rich brownish-red crown with
distinct black and white line through eye to nape.
Slightly curved black bill. Slender whitish legs.
Open country, tank edges, lagoons.
Rare. BrR. LCDZ.

127. **ORIENTAL PRATINCOLE** (Indian Large Pratincole)   Plate 10.7
Peradiga Javalihiniya   පෙරදිග ජවලිහිණියා   *Glareola maldivarum* *

27 cm.
NBr: duller with black border to throat patch
replaced by dark brown streaks.
Open country besides marshes,lagoons.
Rare. BrR. LCDZ.

128. **SMALL PRATINCOLE**   Plate 10.8   *Glareola lactea*
Kuda Javalihiniya   කුඩා ජවලිහිණියා

18 cm.
Open country besides marshes, lagoons, dry river beds.
Rare. BrR. LCDZ.

LARIDAE

129. **GREAT BLACK-HEADED GULL**   Plate 13.2   *Larus ichthyaetus*
Maha hisa-kalu Galuviya   මහ හිස-කළු ගලුවියා

71 cm.
Sea-coast, rivers, tanks, lagoons.
Rare. Migrant. LCDZ. Infrequent visitor WZ.

130. **BROWN-HEADED GULL**   Plate 13.1   *Larus brunnicephalus*
Hisa dumburu Galuviya   හිස දුඹුරු ගලුවියා

45 cm.
Sea-coast, tanks, rivers, lagoons.
Common. Migrant. LC.

131. **GULL-BILLED TERN**   Plate 13.3   *Sterna nilotica**
Galu-hota Muhudu-lihiniya   ගලු-හොට මුහුදු-ලිහිණියා

38 cm.
Sea-coast, marshes, lagoons.
Common. Migrant and resident populations.
Breeding population probably off Mannar (Tallaimannar).
LC.

132. **CASPIAN TERN**   Plate 13.5   *Sterna caspia**
Caspiyanu Muhudu-lihiniya   කැස්පියානු මුහුදු-ලිහිණියා

54 cm.
NBr: white streaks on black cap.
Sea-coast, lagoons.
Common. Migrant and resident populations.
LCDZ. Infrequent visitor WZ.

133. LESSER CRESTED TERN

Sterna bengalensis

Kuda konda Muhudu-lihiniya කුඩා කොණ්ඩ මුහුදු-ලිහිණියා

38 cm.
Crown heavily streaked with white. Black on
head takes shape of 'U'. Yellowish-red
bill and pale grey upper plumage.
Coastal waters, estuaries, lagoons.
Common. Migrant. LC.

134. GREAT CRESTED TERN Plate 13.4

Sterna bergii

Maha konda Muhudu-lihiniya මහ කොණ්ඩ මුහුදු-ලිහිණියා

45 cm.
NBr: white of forehead extends to lores.
White streaks on black crown.
Coastal waters, estuaries, lagoons.
Common. BrR. LC.

135. SANDWICH TERN

Sterna sandvicensis

Sandwich Muhudu-lihiniya සැන්ඩ්විච් මුහුදු-ලිහිණියා

42 cm.
Black bill tipped yellow.
NBr: short black crest. Feet black.
Sea-coast, lagoons.
Rare. Migrant. LCDZ.

136. ROSEATE TERN Plate 13.6

Sterna dougallii

Arunuvan Muhudu-lihiniya අරුණුවන් මුහුදු-ලිහිණියා

33cm.
Sea-coast, lagoons.
Common. Migrant and resident populations (some birds
breed during summer in coral islets off east coast). LC.

137. COMMON TERN

Sterna hirundo

Podu Muhudu-lihiniya පොදු මුහුදු-ලිහිණියා

33 cm.
Grey and white plumage. Tail deeply forked.
Outer tail feathers long. Outer edge of tail often
blackish. Nape black. Leading edge of inner
half of wing-lining blackish. Bill black.
Feet dusky red to black. Tip of tail slightly longer
than end of folded wing.
Br: basal portion of bill becomes red.
Sea-coast, estuaries, marshes, tanks.
Rare. Migrant. LC.

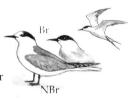

138. **LITTLE TERN**   Plate 13.9   *Sterna albifrons**
Kuda Muhudu-lihiniya   කුඩා මුහුදු-ලිහිණියා

23 cm.
Together with black-shafted Little Tern, the smallest tern in Sri Lanka.
In flight: 2-3 outer primaries black. Pale greyish
upperparts and wings contrasting with white rump.
Sea-coast, estuaries, rivers, lagoons, tanks.
Common. BrR. LCDZ, visits WZ.

139. **BLACK-SHAFTED LITTLE TERN** (Saunder's Tern)
                                                                 *Sterna saundersi**
Saundersge Muhudu-lihiniya   සෝන්ඩර්ස්ගේ මුහුදු-ලිහිණියා

23 cm.
Similar to little tern. Distinguished from
it by 3-7 black outer primaries and grey rump.
Sea-coast, estuaries, lagoons, tanks.
Rare. Migrant. LCDZ.

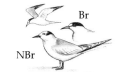

140. **BRIDLED TERN**   Plate 13.10   *Sterna anaethetus*
Piyapath dumburu Muhudu-lihiniya   පියාපත් දුඹුරු මුහුදු-ලිහිණියා

37 cm.
Supercilium extends beyond eye.
NBr: crown and nape region sooty brown.
Open-ocean, islets, estuaries, lagoons, tanks.
Common. Migrant. LCDZ.

141. **SOOTY TERN**   *Sterna fuscata*
Dumbutuvan Muhudu-lihiniya   දුඹුටුවන් මුහුදු-ලිහිණියා

43 cm.
Black upperparts, white underparts. White of forehead
extending up to the eye. Black bill and legs. Forked tail.
NBr: crown and lores streaked with white.
Open-ocean, coast, lagoons.
Very rare. Migrant. LC.

142. **WHISKERED TERN**   Plate 13.7   *Chlidonias hybridus*
Kangul-lihiniya   කාගුල්-ලිහිණියා

28 cm.
NBr: black cap extending on to rear crown and hind neck, but not
below eye, streaky appearance in the region of the forehead.
Marshes, tanks, paddy fields, sea-coast, lagoons.
Very common. Migrant, possibly breeds on islands off the coast. LC.

143. **WHITE-WINGED BLACK TERN** (White-winged Tern)   Plate 13.8
Chlidonias leucopterus

Piyapath sudu Kangul-lihiniya   පියාපත් සුදු තාහුල්-ලිහිණියා

25 cm.
NBr: black patch from crown to ear coverts, extends below eye.
Marshes, tanks, paddy-fields, sea-coast, lagoons.
Rare. Migrant (some resident populations). LC.

COLUMBIDAE

144. **ROCK PIGEON**   *Columba livia*
Gal Paraviya   ගල් පරවියා

33 cm.
Blue-grey.Two broad black bars on wing.
Black bar at tip of tail. Whitish under wing.
Neck darker, glossed with green and
purplish-blue. Black bill. Red feet.
Villages, cultivations, rock islets.
Very rare. BrR. LCDZ.
(Domestic variety very common).

145. **SRI LANKA WOOD-PIGEON**   Plate 14.1   *Columba torringtoni*
Lanka Maila-goya   ලංකා මයිල-ගොයා

35 cm.
Endemic species.
Forest, gardens.
Rare. BrR. HC, descends down to LCWZ during fruiting seasons.

146. **SPOTTED DOVE**   Plate 14.6   *Streptopelia chinensis*
Alu Kobeyiya   අළු කොබෙයියා

30 cm.
Plumage variation from bluish grey in the
DZ to greyish-brown in the WZ.
Open country, cultivated land, gardens.
Very common. BrR. All zones.

147. **RED COLLARD DOVE** (Red Turtle Dove)   *Streptopelia tranquebarica*
Rathu tutura Kobeyiya   රතු පුටුර කොබෙයියා

23 cm.
Short tail and plump body. Outer tail feathers
tipped with white. Wing lining dark grey.
Male: brick-red body and upper wing coverts.
Grey head and throat. Blackish flight feathers.
Black half-ring on hind neck. Lower back and tail
blackish. Under tail coverts white.
Female: brown,very much like Collared Dove,
but with a smaller and shorter tail.
Open country, scrub.
Rare. Migrant. LCDZ (northern region).
Unconfirmed Br reported from Jaffna.

148. **EURASIAN COLLARED DOVE** (Indian Ring Dove)
Mala Kobeyiya   මාල කොබෙයියා   *Streptopelia decaocto*

33 cm.
Pale grey brown bird with a distinct narrow black
half-collar on hind neck. Breast reddish
becoming ashy grey on abdomen.
Darker vent and tail-coverts. White edge to
blackish tail, visible clearly when tail is spread out.
Open country, scrub.
Common. BrR. (North western) LCDZ from Puttlam to Jaffna.

149. **EMERALD DOVE**   (Bronze-winged Pigeon) Plate 14.5
Neela-kobeyiya   නිල-කොබෙයියා   *Chalcophaps indica*

25 cm.
Female: duller, with greyish-whitefore head and blue-grey crown.
Lateral tail feathers reddish-brown.
Forest, wooded gardens (ground bird).
Common. BrR. All zones.

150. **ORANGE-BREASTED GREEN PIGEON**   Plate 14.2
Laya ran Bata goya   ළය රන් බට ගොයා   *Treron bicincta*

25 cm.
Female: green breast. Under tail coverts whitish,
with inner webs of feathers reddish-brown.
Forest, forest edge, scrub.
Common. BrR. LC.

151. **POMPADOUR GREEN-PIGEON** Plate 14.3   *Treron pompadora*
Pompadura Bata goya   පොම්පඩෝර් බට ගොයා

25 cm.
Forest, forest edge, scrub.
Common. BrR. All zones.

152. **YELLOW-FOOTED GREEN-PIGEON** (Yellow-legged Green-Pigeon)
Seepadu Bata goya   සීපාදු බට ගොයා   *Treron phoenicoptera*

23 cm.
Yellowish-green and bright ashy yellow below.
Reddish shoulder patch. Yellow legs.
Distinct band across wing.
Female: duller and shoulder patch fainter.
Forest.

Two subspecies which cannot be distinguished in the field.
Treron phoenicoptera chlorigaster **(Southern Yellow-footed Green-Pigeon).**
Larger bird, wing length greater than 170 mm.
Very rare. Migrant. LCDZ.
Treron phoenicoptera phillipsi **(Yellow-footed Green-Pigeon).**
Smaller bird, wing length less than 170 mm.
Rare. BrR. LCDZ (mostly Uva Province).

153. **GREEN IMPERIAL-PIGEON** Plate 14.4   *Ducula aenea*
Maha Neela-goya   මහා නිල-ගොයා

43 cm.
Forest, forest edge, gardens (confined to the canopy).
Common. BrR. LC.

PSITTACIDAE

154. **SRI LANKA HANGING PARROT** (Lorikeet) Plate 15.5
Lanka Giramaliththa   ලංකා ගිරාමලිත්තා   *Loriculus beryllinus*

14 cm.
Endemic species.
Female: duller than male with only traces of a blue throat patch.
Forest, gardens.
Common. BrR. All zones (mainly foot hills of WZ).

155. **ALEXANDRINE PARAKEET** Plate 15.6   *Psittacula eupatria*
Labu Girawa   ලබු ගිරවා

51 cm.
Forest, cultivations.
Common. BrR. LCDZ, less seen in WZ.

156. **ROSE-RINGED PARAKEET**   Plate 15.8   *Psittacula kramerii*
Rana Girawa   රන ගිරවා

40 cm.
Secondary forest, cultivations, gardens, urban areas.
Very common. BrR. LC.

157. **PLUM-HEADED PARAKEET**   (Blossom-headed Parakeet) Plate 15.4
Pandu Girawa   පඬු ගිරවා   *Psittacula cyanocephala*

34 cm.
Slender white tip to bluish central tail feathers.
Forest, cultivations, gardens.
Common. BrR. All zones (mainly mid-mountains).

158. **SRI LANKA LAYARD'S PARAKEET**   Plate 15.7   *Psittacula calthropae*
Lanka alu Girawa   ලංකා අළු ගිරවා

30 cm.
Endemic species.
Forest, gardens.
Common. BrR. Mainly WZ and forested humid areas of LC.

CUCULIDAE

159. **PIED CUCKOO** (Pied Crested Cuckoo)   Plate 16.1
Gomara Konda-koha   ගෝමර කොණ්ඩ-කොහා   *Oxylophus jacobinus**

35 cm.
Forest, scrubland, cultivations, gardens.
Common. BrR. LC, scarce in WZ.

160. **CHESTNUT-WINGED CUCKOO**   (Red-winged Crested Cuckoo)
Path rathu Konda-koha   පත් රතු කොණ්ඩ-කොහා   *Clamator coromandus*

45 cm.
Distinct black crest. Long tail.
Black upperparts with white nuchal collar.
Reddish-brown wings. Rust coloured chin,
throat and upper breast. Rest of underparts white
or whitish. Black bill and legs.
Forest. Associated with feeding flocks.
Rare. Migrant. LC.

161. **COMMON HAWK CUCKOO**   *Cuculus varius*
Ukusu Kokilaya   උකුසු කෝකිලයා

33 cm.
Ashy grey above. Tail tinged
reddish-brown with four or five whitish and black
bars, the terminal bar broadest. Less distinct
streaking on throat and breast. Underparts white,
tinged with brownish-red and ash on breast.
Brownish bars on abdomen and flanks.
Forest, scrub, cultivations.
Rare. BrR. All zones.

162. **INDIAN CUCKOO**   *Cuculus micropterus*
Indiyanu Kokilaya   ඉන්දියානු කෝ තිලයා

33 cm.
Dark slaty-grey above with a brownish tinge.
Underparts pale ashy and white, cross-barred
broadly with black. Dull greyish green eye ring.
Broad black subterminal band on upper
surface of tail. Distinct call during the months
of February to about early June.
Forest.
Common. Probably BrR (earlier considered a migrant). LCDZ.

163. **LESSER CUCKOO** (Small Cuckoo)   *Cuculus poliocephalus*
Punchi Kokilaya   පුංචි කෝකිලයා

28 cm.
Rump and tail coverts dark and not
contrasting with tail. Black barring on
underparts broad and widely spaced.
Much buffier especially on under tail coverts.
Forest, scrub.
Rare. Migrant. All zones.

164. **BANDED- BAY CUCKOO**   *Cacomantis sonneratii*
Vayira Pingu-koha   වයිර පිඟු-කොහා

23 cm.
Upperparts bright brownish-red with dark
brown cross bars. Pale supercillium.
Underparts whitish with brown barring.
Tail brownish-red, tipped with white and
sub tipped with black.
Forest.
Common. BrR. All zones.

165. **GREY-BELLIED CUCKOO** (Plaintive Cuckoo) Plate 16.2
Lathoni Pingu-koha ලතෝනි පිංගු-කොහා *Cacomantis passerinus**

21 cm.
Hepatic phase of the female lacks a whitish eye-brow and has buffier
sides of head, distinguishing it from the Banded Bay Cuckoo.
The grey phase resembles the male.
Forest.
Common. Migrant. All zones.

166. **DRONGO CUCKOO** *Surniculus lugubris*
Kavudu-koha කවුඩු-කොහා

23 cm.
Entirely black with slightly forked tail.
White bars on under tail coverts and outer tail
feathers. The feeding behaviour and the
shape of the beak enable it to be distinguished
from drongos.
Forest, scrub.
Rare. BrR. LC.

167. **ASIAN KOEL** Plate 16.4 *Eudynamys scolopacea*
Koha කොහා

43 cm.
Forest. Mostly in proximity to human habitation.
Very common. BrR. LC.

168. **BLUE-FACED MALKOHA** Plate 16.5 *Phaenicophaeus viridirostris*
Watha nil Malkoha වත නිල් මල්කොහා

39 cm.
Forest.
Common. BrR. LCDZ (rarely in drier edges of the WZ).

169. **SIRKEER MALKOHA** (Southern Sirkeer) *Phaenicophaeus leschenaultii**
Pathan-atikukula පතන-ඇටිකුකුළා

43 cm.
Sandy brown plumage.
Long tail with white tipped lateral tail-feathers.
Bright red to yellow-red bill.
Black streaks on head and breast feathers.
Forest.
Rare. BrR. LCDZ, Uva sub-montane area up to Maduru Oya.

170. **RED-FACED MALKOHA** Plate 16.3   *Phaenicophaeus pyrrhocephalus*
Watha rathu Malkoha වත රතු මල්කොහා

45 cm.
Endemic species (but sighted in Kerala? See C. H. Biddulph (1969).,
JBNHS 53:697-81).
Female: irides white.
Male: irides brown.
Confined to undisturbed forest areas in the wet zone and
riverine forests of the dry zone.
Rare. BrR. All zones.

171. **GREATER COUCAL** Plate 16.7   *Centropus sinensis*
Ati-kukula අටි-කුකුළා

48 cm.
Forest, residential areas.
Very common. BrR. All zones.

172. **SRI LANKA GREEN-BILLED COUCAL** Plate 16.6
Lanka bata Ati-kukula ලංකා බට අටි-කුකුළා   *Centropus chlororhynchus*

43 cm.
Endemic species.
Undisturbed forests. Associated with bamboo and cane rushes.
Very rare. BrR. LCWZ.

TYTONIDAE

173. **BARN OWL**   *Tyto alba*
Atu-bakamuna අටු-බකමුණා

34 cm. Upperparts golden-buff and grey, spotted with
black and white. Underparts white with buff tinge and
dark brown spots. Heart shaped white facial-disc.
Cultivated land.
Rare. BrR. LCDZ - north western coastal strip.

174. **ORIENTAL BAY -OWL**   *Phodilus badius*
Mukalan-bassa මුකලන්-බස්සා

29 cm.
Upperparts reddish-brown, spotted
with black and buff. Facial disc margined
with white and a little black. Reddish-brown
around eyes. Tail reddish-brown, barred with
black. Irides dark brown.
Forest.
Rare. BrR. LCWZ and HC.

175. **ORIENTAL SCOPS-OWL** (Little Scops-owl)   Plate 17.4   *Otus sunia* *
Singithi Bassa   සිඟිති බස්සා

19 cm.
Forest, gardens.
Rare. BrR. All zones.

176. **INDIAN SCOPS-OWL**   (Collared Scops-owl)   Plate 17.2
Kan-diga Bassa   කන්-දිග බස්සා   *Otus bakkamoena*

23 cm.
Forest, gardens.
Common. BrR. All zones.

177. **SPOT-BELLIED EAGLE-OWL** (Forest Eagle-0wl)   Plate 17.5
Ulama   උලමා   *Bubo nipalensis*

61 cm.
This is the so-called "Devil bird," known to make
"dreadful shrieks and strangulating noises" (Henry, 1971).
Forest.
Rare. BrR. All zones.

178. **BROWN FISH-OWL**   Plate 17.1   *Ketupa zeylonensis**
Dumburu Kevul-bakamuna   දුඹුරු කෙවුල්-බකමුණා

54 cm.
Forest. Close to water bodies.
Common. BrR. All zones.

179. **BROWN WOOD-OWL**   *Strix leptogrammica*
Dumburu Wana-bakamuna   දුඹුරු වන-බකමුණා

40-56 cm.
Brown, closely barred upperparts.
White throat, rest of underparts buffy white
with narrow chocolate-brown bars.
Light brownish-red facial disc.
Whitish eye ring. Broad black ring round
margin of facial disc. Brown eyes.
Forest.
Common. BrR. All zones.

180. JUNGLE OWLET

*Glaucidium radiatum**

Wayira Wana-bassa වයිර වන-බස්සා

20 cm.
Upperparts dark brown closely barred with
brownish-buff. Underparts, chin,
moustachial streak, middle of breast and
abdomen white. Rest barred dark
yellowish-green, brown and white.
In flight : brownish-red patch on underwing.
Forest, scrub, cultivations.
Common. BrR. LCDZ, less in WZ.

181. SRI LANKA CHESTNUT-BACKED OWLET Plate 64.3

*Glaucidium castanonotus**

Lanka pitathambala Wana-bassa ලංකා පිටතඹල වන-බස්සා

20 cm.
Endemic species.
Reddish brown, barred with reddish brown-buff.
Underparts, chin, moustachial streak, middle of breast and abdomen
white. Rest barred dark yellowish-brown and white.
In flight : reddish brown patch on underwing.
Forest, scrub, cultivations.
Rare. BrR. LCWZ and HC.

182. BROWN HAWK-OWL

Ninox scutulata

Dumburu Ukusu-bassa දුඹුරු උකුසු-බස්සා

30 cm.
Looks like a stocky hawk, with broad round
wings. No facial disc. Upperparts dark brown.
White patches between eyes and hidden spots on
wing. Underparts buffy to white with broad
reddish-brown streaks. Irides yellow. Tail barred.
Forest, cultivations.
Common. BrR. All zones.

183. SHORT-EARED OWL

Asio flammeus

Kan kota Bakamuna කන් කොට බකමුණා

38 cm.
Very small "ears," not very visible in the field.
Upperparts mottled and streaked
blackish and buff on brown.
Underparts buff, streaked with black.
Head dark greyish, whitish facial disc. Yellow irides.
Forest, scrub.
Rare . Migrant. All zones.

PODARGIDAE

184. FROGMOUTH Plate 17.6   *Batrachostomus monilieger*
Madi-muhuna මැටි-මුහුණා

23 cm.
Female: reddish-brown, spotted with black and white.
Forest.
Rare. BrR. All zones.

CAPRIMULGIDAE

185. GREY NIGHTJAR (Highland Nightjar)   *Caprimulgus indicus*
Kandurata Bimbassa කඳුරට බිම්බස්සා

28 cm.
Grey-brown plumage with buff and black
markings.
Male: white spots on the four outer pairs of tail
feathers. Buff ear coverts.
Female: lacks white tips of tail and the white on the primaries are buff.
Forest.
Rare. BrR. HC.

186. JERDON'S NIGHTJAR (Horsefield's Jungle Nightjar)
Dikpenda Bimbassa දික්පෙද බිම්බස්සා   *Caprimulgus atripennis**

30 cm.
Greyish-brown, marked with black and buff.
Male: prominent white patch on tips of outer
two tail feathers. Collar dull rusty.Throat whitish.
Underparts with dark brown bars.
Female: white patch on primaries.
Outer tail feather patches small and buff.
Forest.
Common. BrR. All zones, mainly in the DZ.

187. COMMON NIGHTJAR (Common Southern Nightjar) Plate 17.7
Podu Bimbassa පොදු බිම්බස්සා   *Caprimulgus asiaticus*
23 cm.
Forest.
Common. BrR. All zones, mostly in LCDZ.

APODIDAE

188. **INDIAN SWIFTLET** (Edible-nest Swift)   Plate 20.1
Indiyanu Kadal-thurithaya   ඉන්දියානු කැදැල්-තුරිතයා   *Collocalia unicolor**

13 cm.
Open country, coastal and rocky areas.
Common. BrR. All zones.

189. **BROWN-BACKED NEEDLETAIL**   (Brown-throated Spinetail)
Plate 20.4   *Hirundapus giganteus**
Katupenda-thurithaya   කටුපෙද-තුරිතයා

23 cm.
Forest, open ground.
Rare. Status uncertain.
Probably BrR. Lower HC (occasionally in other areas).

190. **ASIAN PALM-SWIFT**   Plate 20.2   *Cypsiurus balasiensis**
Thal-thurithaya   තල්-තුරිතයා

13 cm.
Found in areas with palm trees.
Common. BrR. All zones.

191. **ALPINE SWIFT**   *Tachymarptis melba**
Sethodara-thurithaya   සේතෝදර-තුරිතයා

22 cm.
Brown above. Underparts white with dark
pectoral band across breast.
Brown undertail coverts.
Large pointed wings.
Rocky areas, over paddy fields, canals.
Rare. BrR. HC. Visitor LC.

192. **LITTLE SWIFT** (House Swift)   Plate 20.3   *Apus affinis*
Katiya sudu Thurithaya   කටිය සුදු තුරිතයා

15 cm.
Forest, open areas, close to water, buildings.
Common. BrR. All zones.

HEMIPROCNIDAE

193. CRESTED TREE-SWIFT   Plate 20.7   *Hemiprocne coronata**
Silu Ruk-thurithaya   සිළු රුක්-තුරිතයා

23 cm.
Female: reddish-brown cheek area of male, blackish.
Forest (mainly edges).
Common. BrR. All zones.

TROGONIDAE

194. MALABAR TROGON   Plate 23.2   *Harpactes fasciatus*
Lohawannichchiya   ලෝහවන්නිච්චියා

30 cm.
Humid forests.
Common. BrR. All zones.

ALCEDINIDAE

195. COMMON KINGFISHER   Plate 18.5   *Alcedo atthis*
Podu Mal-pilihuduwa   පොදු මල්-පිළිහුඩුවා

18 cm.
Close to water.
Very common. BrR. All zones.

196. BLUE-EARED KINGFISHER   Plate 18.6   *Alcedo meninting*
Nila karni Mal-pilihuduwa   නිල කර්ණි මල්-පිළිහුඩුවා

15 cm.
Close to water in forest.
Very rare. BrR. LCDZ (most records from the lower Uva
foothils around Nilgala).

197. BLACK-BACKED KINGFISHER (Three-toed Kingfisher)   Plate 18.1
Ran-pilihuduwa   රන්-පිළිහුඩුවා   *Ceyx erithacus*

13 cm.
Humid forest.
Rare. BrR. All zones.

198. STORK-BILLED KINGFISHER   Plate 18.2   *Pelargopsis capensis*
Manathudu Maha-pilihuduwa   මානාතුඩු මහ-පිළිහුඩුවා

38 cm.
Marshes, mangorves, rivers, swamp forest.
Common. BrR. LC, recent records from mid country.

199. **WHITE-THROATED KINGFISHER**   Plate 18.4
(White-breasted Kingfisher)   *Halcyon smyrnensis*
Laya sudu Pilihuduwa   ලය සුදු පිළිහුඩුවා

28 cm.
Open areas near water, gardens, towns.
Very common. BrR. All zones.

200. **BLACK-CAPPED KINGFISHER** Plate 18.3
(Black-capped Purple Kingfisher)   *Halcyon pileata*
Hisa Kalu Dam-pilihuduwa   හිස කළු දම්-පිළිහුඩුවා

30 cm.
Mangroves,lagoons,tanks, streams.
Rare. Migrant. LC.

201. **PIED KINGFISHER**   Plate 18.7   *Ceryle rudis*
Gomara Kalapu-pilihuduwa   ගෝමර කළපු-පිළිහුඩුවා

30 cm.
Female: the lower breast band of the male absent.
The upper band interrupted in the center.
Marshes, rivers, mangroves, tanks.
Common. BrR. LC.

MEROPIDAE

202. **LITTLE GREEN BEE-EATER** (Green Bee-eater)   Plate 15.1
Palavan Binguharaya   පළාවන් බිඟුහරයා   *Merops orientalis*

20 cm.
Open country, forest edge, forest.
Very common. BrR. LCDZ. Occasional visitor WZ.

203. **BLUE-TAILED BEE-EATER**   Plate 15.2   *Merops philippinus*
Penda nil Binguharaya   පෙඳනිල් බිඟුහරයා

30 cm.
Marshes, open country, forest.
Very common.
Migrant (small breeding population at Kumana in the south-east).
All zones.

204. **CHESTNUT-HEADED BEE-EATER**   Plate 15.3   *Merops leschenaulti*
Pinguhis Binguharaya   පිඟුහිස් බිඟුහරයා

17 cm.
Open country, forest. Found in small numbers,
often in the high canopy.
Common. BrR. All zones.

CORACIIDAE

205. **INDIAN ROLLER** Plate 22.4
Dumbonna දුම්බොන්නා

33 cm.
Open country, cities.
Common. BrR. LC (commoner in the DZ).

Coracias benghalensis

206. **DOLLARBIRD** (Broad-billed Roller)
Dumkava දුම්කාවා

30 cm.
Dusky bluish green plumage.
Bright blue wings. Large white patch on primaries,
distinct in flight. Broad, orange-red bill and legs.
At rest, the bird appears black.
Forest. Commonly sighted high up on dead trees
close to openings in the forest.
Very rare. BrR. LC.

Eurystomus orientalis

UPUPIDAE

207. **EURASIAN HOOPOE** Plate 22.7
Poroluva පොරොවා

30 cm.
Scrub, open forest.
Rare. BrR. LCDZ, rarely in HC.

Upupa epops

BUCEROTIDAE

208. **SRI LANKA GREY HORNBILL** Plate 22.6
Alu Kandaththa අළු කැඳැත්තා

59 cm.
Endemic species.
Female: bill dull black with a long cream patch on
the side of the upper mandible.
Forest.
Very common. BrR. LC, visitor to HC.

Ocyceros gingalensis*

209. MALABAR PIED HORNBILL Plate 22.5   *Anthracoceros coronatus*
Poro-kandaththa   පොරෝ-කැඳැත්තා

61 cm.
Male: black at gape extends to upper mandible.
Less white around eye. Posterior edge of casque black.
Forest, open areas. Roosts in large numbers in the
non-breeding season.
Common. BrR. LCDZ.

CAPITONIDAE

210. BROWN-HEADED BARBET Plate 21.3   *Megalaima zeylanica*
Polos Kottoruwa   පොළොස් කොට්ටෝරුවා

26 cm.
Forest, home gardens.
Very common. BrR. All zones.

211. SRI LANKA YELLOW-FRONTED BARBET Plate 21.6
Rannalal Kottoruwa   රන්නලල් කොට්ටෝරුවා   *Megalaima flavifrons*

22 cm.
Endemic species.
Forest, home gardens.
Very common. BrR. WZ, mostly HC.

212. CRIMSON-FRONTED BARBET (Small Barbet) Plate 21.5
Oluwa rathu Kottoruwa   ඔළුව රතු කොට්ටෝරුවා   *Megalaima rubricapilla*

14 cm.
Forest, gardens.
Very common. BrR. All zones.

213. COPPERSMITH BARBET (Crimson Breasted Barbet) Plate 21.4
                                                          Megalaima haemacephala
Botuwa rathu Kottoruwa   බොටුව රතු කොට්ටෝරුවා

15 cm.
Forest, gardens.
Common. BrR. LCDZ and lower HC.

PICIDAE

214. **BROWN-CAPPED WOODPECKER** Plate 19.6
(Pygmy-Woodpecker)
Kuru Gomara-karala කුරු ගෝමර-කැරලා

Dendrocopos nanus

13 cm.
Female: red occipital streak absent.
Forest, cultivation, gardens.
Common. BrR. All zones.

215. **YELLOW-CROWNED WOODPECKER**   Plate 19.5
(Yellow-fronted Pied Woodpecker)
Pithagra Gomara-kerala පිතාග්‍ර ගෝමර-කැරලා   *Dendrocopos mahrattensis*

19 cm.
Forest.
Common. BrR. LCDZ (common in the south east) and HC (rare).

216. **RUFOUS WOODPECKER**   *Celeus brachyurus**
Rathudumburu Koda-kerala රතුදුඹුරු කොඩ-කැරලා

25 cm.
Plumage, brown with a red-brown tinge.
Narrow black bars on upperparts.
Underparts often barred similarly.
Black bill. No crest.
Male: small crimson patch under the eye.
Forest, cultivations.
Rare. BrR. All zones.

217. **LESSER YELLOWNAPE** Plate 19.4
(Lesser Yellow-naped Woodpecker)   *Picus chlorolophus*
Peetha pitakara Kola-kerala පිත පිටකර කොළ-කැරලා

20 cm.
Forest. Follows "feeding flocks".
Common. BrR. All zones.

218. **STREAK THROATED WOODPECKER**   Plate 19.3
(Small Scaly-bellied Woodpecker)   *Picus xanthopygaeus**
Korala udara Kola-kerala කොරළ උදර කොළ-කැරලා

29 cm.
Forest.
Rare. BrR. LCDZ and HC (sub-montane).

219. **BLACK-RUMPED FLAMEBACK**   Plate 19.1
(Golden-Backed Woodpecker)   *Dinopium benghalense*
Two subspecies.
Dinopium benghalense jaffnense
BLACK-RUMPED FLAMEBACK (Golden-backed Woodpecker)
Pita ran Rath-kerala   පිට රන් රත්-කැරලා

28 cm.
Forest, cultivations.
Common. BrR. LCDZ northern region.

Dinopium benghalense psarodes
RED-BACKED WOODPECKER
Pita Rathu Rath-kerala   පිට රතු රත්-කැරලා

28 cm.
Forest, cultivations.
Very common. BrR. All zones (except LCDZ northern region).

220. **GREATER FLAMEBACK** (Crimson-backed Woodpecker) Plate 19.2
Pita levan Maha-kerala   පිට ලේවන් මහ-කැරලා   *Chrysocolaptes lucidus*

33 cm.
Forest, cultivations.
Rare. BrR. All zones.

221. **WHITE-NAPED WOODPECKER** (Black-backed Yellow Woodpecker)
Pita kaha Maha-kerala   පිට කහ මහ-කැරලා   *Chrysocolaptes festivus*

31 cm.
Lower back, tail and sides of head, black. Golden
green on uppersurface of wings. White stripe
starting from either side of neck forming a large V-
shaped white patch on upper and middle back. White
line below eye from base of bill to breast region.
Crown with red crest. Under parts of chin, throat and
foreneck white with fine narrow black longitudinal
streaks. Rest of underparts creamy white.
Female: golden yellow crest.
Forest, cultivations.
Rare. BrR. LCDZ (south eastern and northern region).

PITTIDAE

222. **INDIAN PITTA**   Plate 23.7
Avichchiya   අවිච්චියා   *Pitta brachyura*
19 cm.
In flight: more blue visible. Bill black.
Forests, gardens.
Common. Migrant. All zones.

223. **RUFOUS-WINGED LARK** (Bushlark)   Plate 30.7   *Mirafra assamica*
Akul Thulikava අකුල් තුළිකාවා

15 cm.
Frequently flies in the air to a height and then "parachutes"
down singing all the while. At take off, always crouches down fully.
Heavy bill.
Open country, paddy fields, grassy areas.
Very common. BrR. LC.

224. **ASHY-CROWNED SPARROW-LARK** (Finch-Lark)

Eremopterix grisea

Kalu udara Salika-thulikava කළු උදර සළිකා-තුළිකාවා

13 cm.
Sparrow-like but shorter stance.
Male: pale grey to sandy brown plumage.
Brownish black chin, breast, abdomen and
line through the eye. Brown cap, white
cheeks and side of breast. Black bill.
Female: very much like house sparrow, but greyer.
Open country, grasslands, dry paddy fields.
Common. BrR. LCDZ. Common in the more arid regions.

225. **ORIENTAL SKYLARK**   *Alauda gulgula*
Guvan Thulikava ගුවන් තුළිකාවා

16 cm.
Similar to Bush Lark but greyer, slightly
smaller. Long tail. Upperparts brown with dark
streaks. Underparts brownish buff with streaks on
breast. Wing is greyer. Lacks brownish-red nature.
White outer tail feathers. Grey collar behind ear
coverts. When excited erects small crest of feathers
on forehead.
Open country, grassland, cultivation.
Common. BrR. LCDZ, and HC.

HIRUNDINIDAE

226. **BARN SWALLOW** Plate 20.6   *Hirundo rustica*
Wahi-lihiniya වැහි-ලිහිණියා

15 cm.
Open areas (often near water), cities, villages.
Numerous subspecies based on colour variations.
Often difficult to separate.
Plate depicts most common subspecies (*H. rustica guttralis*).
Very common. Migrant. All zones.

227. **HILL SWALLOW**   *Hirundo dumicola**
Kandukara Wahi-lihiniya කඳුකර වැහි-ලිහිණියා

14 cm.
Upperparts bright dark blue. Larger patch of
brownish-red on forehead. Underparts
brownish-red, extending to upper breast.
No dark breast band. Rest of underparts
brownish grey to white. Outer tail feathers shorter.
Open grasslands, villages, towns.
Common. BrR. HC, visitor to LCWZ.

228. **RED-RUMPED SWALLOW** Plate 20.8   *Hirundo daurica*
Rathu kati Wahi-lihiniya රතු කටි වැහි-ලිහිණියා

18 cm.
Open areas.
Three subspecies have been recorded, of which the most common is
Hirundo daurica hyperythra, with dark reddish-brown underparts.
Common. BrR. All zones.

LANIIDAE

229. **BROWN /PHILIPPINE SHRIKE** Plate 24.5/6   *Lanius cristatus*
Dumburu/Pilipina Sabarittha දුඹුරු/පිලිපීන සබරිත්තා

19 cm.
Open country, forest, scrub. The prey searching habit of perching on a
vantage point above the vegetation and calling is characteristic.

Two subspecies:
Lanius cristatus cristatus **(Brown Shrike)** (Plate 24.5)
Common. Migrant. All zones.
Lanius cristatus lucionensis **(Philippine Shrike)** (Plate 24.6)
Very rare. Migrant. All zones.

230. **LONG-TAILED SHRIKE** (Rufous-rumped Shrike)   Plate 24.1
Rathu kati Sabarittha   රතු කටි සබරිත්තා   *Lanius schach*

25 cm.
Open country, forest, scrub.
Common. BrR. LCDZ (north western coastal strip north of Puttlam).

ORIOLIDAE

231. **EURASIAN GOLDEN ORIOLE**   *Oriolus oriolus*
Ran Kahakurulla   රන් කහකුරුල්ලා

25 cm.
Male: general plumage bright yellow with black
on wing, tail and lores.
Bill and irides reddish-yellow.
Female: greenish yellow above.
Upperparts and underparts streaked with black.
Bill and eyes red.
Black streak across eye faint. Rump pale yellow.
Forest, gardens.

Two subspecies:
Oriolus oriolus oriolus (**European Golden Oriole**).
Black of lores not extending behind eye.
Very rare. Migrant. LCDZ. One specimen (Ripley, 1944,: 409).
Oriolus oriolus kundoo (**Indian Golden Oriole**).
Black of lores extending behind eye.
Rare. Migrant. LC. Mainly Jaffna Penninsula.

232. **BLACK-NAPED ORIOLE**   *Oriolus chinensis*
Pitihisa kalu Kahakurulla   පිටිහිස කළු කහකුරුල්ලා

25 cm.
General plumage bright yellow with black
on wing, tail and from eye to eye across nape.
Bill and eyes red.
Forests, gardens, coastal scrub.
Very rare. Migrant. LC.
Two specimens (pair), and a few sightings in the north.

233. **BLACK-HOODED ORIOLE** (Black-headed Oriole)   Plate 23.6
Hisa Kalu Kahakurulla   හිස කළු කහකුරුල්ලා   *Oriolus xanthornus*

25 cm.
Forest, gardens, cultivations.
Very common. BrR. All zones.

234. BLACK DRONGO
Kalu Kauda   කළු කවුඩා

Dicrurus macrocercus*

28 cm.
Dull black plumage. Slender build. Tail forked.
Outer tail feathers not very long and only
slightly upturned at tip.
No crest on forehead.
Open country, forest, scrub.
Common. BrR. LCDZ (mostly northern region).

235. ASHY DRONGO (Grey Drongo)
Alu paha Kauda   අළු පැහැ කවුඩා

Dicrurus leucophaeus

28 cm.
Plumage dark grey to pale grey.
Above darker than below.
Deeply forked tail.
Crimson eyes.
Forest, scrub.
Rare. Migrant.
LC (more plentiful in the East).

236. WHITE-BELLIED DRONGO (White-vented Drongo)   Plate 22.1
Podu Kauda   පොදු කවුඩා   *Dicrurus caerulescens*

24 cm.
Open country, forest, gardens.

Two subspecies.
Dicrurus caerulescens insularis **(White-bellied Drongo).**
Underparts white from lower breast.
Very common. BrR. LCDZ and HC.
Dicrurus caerulescens leucopygialis **(Dark White-bellied Drongo).**
White restricted to vent area.
Very common. BrR. LCWZ.

237. **GREATER RACKET-TAILED DRONGO**   Plate 22.2 / 3

Dicrurus paradiseus

30-35 cm.
Forest.

Two subspecies.
Dicrurus paradiseus ceylonicus **(Racket-tailed Drongo)**   Plate 22.3
Kalu pithipenda Kauda   කළු පිතිපෙද කවුඩා

Raquet in tail.
Common. BrR. LCDZ.

Dicrurus paradiseus lophorhinus **(Crested Drongo)**   Plate 22.2
Kalu silu Kauda   කළු සිළු කවුඩා

No raquet in tail.
Common. BrR. LCWZ and HC.

ARTAMIDAE

238. **ASHY WOOD SWALLOW-SHRIKE**   Plate 20.5   *Artamus fuscus*
Alu Sabara-lihiniya   අළු සබර-ලිහිණියා

18 cm.
Open country, often seen on power lines above paddy fields.
Common. BrR. All zones.

STURNIDAE

239. **SRI LANKA WHITE-FACED STARLING**
(White-Headed Starling)   Plate 23.1   *Sturnus senex*
Lanka hisa-sudu Sharikava   ලංකා හිස-සුදු ශාරිකාවා

21 cm.
Endemic species.
Juvenile: irides brownish.
Forest.
Rare. BrR. LCWZ and HC.

240. **BRAHMINY STARLING** (Brahminy Mynah)   *Sturnus pagodarum*
Bamunu Sharikava   බමුණු ශාරිකාවා

21 cm.
Open country, scrub forest.
Rare. BrR.
Also migrant population. LCDZ.

241. **ROSY STARLING**   *Sturnus roseus*
Rosa Sharikava   රෝස ශාරිකාවා

23 cm.
Head, neck, upper breast and tail black to grayish.
Rest of plumage rose pink. Crest present.
Grassland, garden, forest.
Very rare. Migrant. LC.

242. **COMMON MYNAH**   Plate 23.8   *Acridotheres tristis*
Myna   මයිනා

23 cm.
Grassland, cities, villages, forest edges close to human habitation.
Very common. BrR. All zones.

243. **SRI LANKA MYNAH** (Sri Lanka Grackle)   Plate 23.5
Lanka Salalihiniya   ලංකා සැලලිහිණියා   *Gracula ptilogenys*

25 cm.
Endemic species.
Forest.
Common. BrR. LCWZ and HC.

244. **HILL MYNAH** (Common Grackle)   Plate 23.4   *Gracula religiosa*
Podu Salalihiniya   පොදු සැලලිහිණියා

25 cm.
Forest.
Common. BrR. All zones.

CORVIDAE

245. **SRI LANKA BLUE MAGPIE**   Plate 23.3   *Urocissa ornata**
Lanka Kahibella   ලංකා කැහිබෙල්ලා

43 cm.
Endemic species.
Forest.
Rare. BrR. LCWZ and HC.

246. **HOUSE CROW**   *Corvus splendens*
Colamba Kaka   කොළඹ කාක්කා

40 cm.
Plumage completely black with grey
collar and upper breast. Cities, rail stations,
associated with human habitation.
Very common. BrR. All zones.

247. **LARGE-BILLED CROW** (Jungle Crow)   *Corvus macrorhynchos*
Kalu Kaputa කළු කපුටා

48 cm.
Glossy black plumage. Large heavy bill.
Town, village, forest.
Very common. BrR. All zones.

CAMPEPHAGIDAE

248. **LARGE CUCKOO-SHRIKE** Plate 24.2   *Coracina macei**
Maha Kovul-saratittha මහ කොවුල්-සැරටිත්තා

30 cm.
Female: lighter face mask, paler plumage.
Forest.
Common. BrR. LCDZ and HC (sub-montane).

249. **BLACK-HEADED CUCKOO-SHRIKE** Plate 24.3   *Coracina melanoptera*
Hisa kalu Kovul-saratittha හිස කළු කොවුල්-සැරටිත්තා

19 cm.
Female: distinct supercillium.
Forest, scrub.
Rare. BrR. All zones.

250. **COMMON WOOD-SHRIKE** Plate 24.4   *Tephrodornis pondicerianus*
Wana-saratittha වන-සැරටිත්තා

14 cm.
Forest, garden, scrub.
Very common BrR. All zones (mainly DZ).

251. **SMALL MINIVET** Plate 21.2   *Pericrocotus cinnamomeus*
Kuda Minivittha කුඩා මිණිවිත්තා

16 cm.
Forest, gardens.
Common. BrR. All zones.

252. **SCARLET MINIVET** (Orange Minivet) Plate 21.1
Maha Minivittha මහ මිණිවිත්තා   *Pericrocotus flammeus*

20 cm.
Forest.
Common. BrR. All zones.

253. **BAR-WINGED FLYCATCHER-SHRIKE** (Pied Shrike)   Plate 24.7
Gomara Kalu-saratittha   ගෝම්බර කළු-සැරටිත්තා   *Hemipus picatus*

15 cm.
Forest, gardens.
Common. BrR. All zones.

IRENIDAE

254. **COMMON IORA**   Plate 21.8   *Aegithina tiphia*
Iorava   අයෝරාවා

15 cm.
Forest, gardens.
Very common. BrR. All zones.

255. **ASIAN FAIRY BLUEBIRD**   *Irena puella*
Nila Rajaya   නිල රාජයා

27 cm.
Male: brilliant dark sea-blue and black above.
Underparts black. Under tail coverts blue.
Female: brown and dull sea blue green,
except flight feathers which are black.
Forest.
Very rare. Migrant. HC.

256. **BLUE-WINGED LEAFBIRD** (Jerdon's Chloropsis)   Plate 21.7
Jerdonge Kolarisiya   ජර්දාන්ගේ කොළරිසියා   *Chloropsis cochinchinensis*

18 cm.
Forest, gardens.
Common. BrR. All zones.

257. **GOLDEN-FRONTED LEAFBIRD**   *Chloropsis aurifrons*
Ran alika Kolarisiya   රන් අලික කොළරිසියා

19 cm.
Plumage completely green.
Golden forehead.
Bluish throat with black border, extending,
beyond the eye.
Bluish patch on shoulder.
Forest, garden.
Rare. BrR. All zones.

258. **BLACK-CRESTED BULBUL** (Black-capped Bulbul)   Plate 25.2
Hisa kalu Kondaya   හිස කළු කොණ්ඩයා   *Pycnonotus melanicterus*

19 cm.
Forest, gardens.
Common. BrR. All zones.

259. **RED-VENTED BULBUL**   Plate 25.6   *Pycnonotus cafer*
Kondaya   කොණ්ඩයා

20 cm.
Forest, gardens, scrub.
Very common. BrR. All zones.

260. **SRI LANKA YELLOW-EARED BULBUL**   Plate 25.4
Pycnonotus penicillatus
Lanka peetha-kan Kondaya   ලංකා පීත-කන්‌ කොණ්ඩයා

20 cm.
Endemic Species.
Forest, gardens close to forest.
Common. BrR. HC.

261. **WHITE-BROWED BULBUL**   Plate 25.3   *Pycnonotus luteolus*
Bama-sudu Kondaya   බැම-සුදු කොණ්ඩයා

20 cm.
A noisy bird with a rolling call.
Secondary forests, scrub, cultivation, gardens.
Very common. BrR. All zones.

262. **YELLOW-BROWED BULBUL**   Plate 25.5   *Iole indica* *
Bama-kaha Guluguduwa   බැම-කහ ගුළුගුඩුවා

20 cm.
Forest, gardens close to forest.

Two subspecies, indistinguishable in the field.
Iole indica guglielmi **(Ceylon Yellow-browed Bulbul)**.
"More greenish on upperparts, yellow on underparts
tinged with green."
Common. BrR. LCWZ.

Iole indica indicus **(Indian Yellow-browed Bulbul).**
"Richer in color especially on sides of head."
Common. BrR LCDZ and HC.

263. **BLACK BULBUL**   Plate 25.1   *Hypsipetes leucocephalus**
Kalu-kondaya   කළු-කොණ්ඩයා

23 cm.
Forest. Frequents the canopy.
Common. BrR. LCWZ and HC, visitor LCDZ.

MUSCICAPIDAE

TIMALINAE

264. **BROWN-CAPPED BABBLER**   Plate 26.8   *Pellorneum fuscocapillum*
Lanka Mudun Bora-demalichcha   ලංකා මුදුන් බොර-දෙමළිච්චා

15 cm.
Endemic species.
Forest under growth, scrub.

Three subspecies.
Pellorneun fuscocapillum babaulti **(Pale Brown-capped Babbler)**.
"Crown dull yellow (fulvous) with chocolate brown tips. Pale plumage"
Common. BrR. LCDZ.
Pellorneum fuscocapillum fuscocapillum **(Brown-capped Babbler).**
"Crown chocolate brown. dark plumage."
Common. BrR. HC.
Pellorneun fuscocapillum scortillum **(Dusky Brown-capped Babbler).**
"Crown chocolate brown. Very dark plumage"
Common. BrR. LCWZ and hills in the south west.

265. **SCIMITAR BABBLER**   Plate 26.4   *Pomatorhinus horsfieldii**
Da-demalichcha   දෑ-දෙමළිච්චා

22 cm.
Forest, undergrowth.

Two subspecies.
Pomatorhinus horsfieldii holdsworthi **(Common Scimitar Babbler).**
"Upperparts Olive-brown"
Common. BrR. LCDZ and HC.
Pomatorhinus horsfieldii melanurus **(Southern Scimitar Babbler).**
"Upperparts bright brownish-red".
Common. BrR. LCWZ.

266. **TAWNY-BELLIED BABBLER** (White-throated Babbler)   Plate 26.6
Dumetia hyperythra

Gela sudu Landu-demalichcha   ගෙල සුදු ලඳු-දෙමළිච්චා

13 cm.
Scrub, tall grassland.
Rare. BrR. All zones.

267. **DARK-FRONTED BABBLER** (Black Fronted Babbler)   Plate 26.7
Rhopocichla atriceps

Hisa kalu Panduru-demalichcha   හිස කළු පඳුරු-දෙමළිච්චා

10 cm.
Forest, scrub, undergrowth.

Two subspecies, indistinguishable in the field.
Rhopocichla atriceps siccatus **(Common Black-fronted Babbler).**
"Upperparts greenish tawny brown (olivaceous-fulvous)."
Common. BrR. DZ.
Rhopocichla atriceps nigrifrons **(Southern Black-fronted Babbler).**
Upperparts reddish tawny brown ("rusty-fulvous").
Common. BrR. WZ.

268. **YELLOW-EYED BABBLER**   Plate 26.5   *Chrysomma sinense*

Peethakshi Thana-demalichcha   පීතාක්ෂි තණ-දෙමළිච්චා

18 cm.
Commonly moves around in pairs.
Scrub, tall grassland.
Rare. BrR. All zones.

269. **SRI LANKA ORANGE-BILLED BABBLER**   Plate 26.3
(Rufous Babbler)
Rathu-demalichcha   රතු-දෙමළිච්චා   *Turdoides rufescens*

25 cm.
Endemic species.
Forest, forest edge.
Common. BrR. LCWZ and HC.

270. **YELLOW-BILLED BABBLER** (Common Babbler)   Plate 26.1

Demalichcha   දෙමළිච්චා   *Turdoides affinis*

23 cm.
Close to human habitation, scrub.
Very common. BrR. All zones.

271. **ASHY-HEADED LAUGHING-THRUSH** (Ashy-headed Babbler)
Plate 26.2 *Garrulax cinereifrons*
Alu-demalichcha අළු-දෙමලිච්චා

25 cm.
Endemic species.
Forest. Frequently seen feeding on the ground.
Rare. BrR. LCWZ and HC.

MUSCICAPINAE

272. **ASIAN BROWN FLYCATCHER** Plate 27.1 *Muscicapa dauurica* *
Dumburu Masimara දුඹුරු මැසිමාරා

13 cm.
Forest, shady areas in gardens, close to human habitation.
Common. Migrant. All zones.

273. **BROWN-BREASTED FLYCATCHER** (Layard's Flycatcher) Plate 27.2
Laya dumburu Masimara ලය දුඹුරු මැසිමාරා *Muscicapa muttui*

14 cm.
Forest, close to residences.
Humid locations
Rare. Migrant. All zones.

274. **KASHMIR FLYCATCHER** (Kashmir Red-breasted Flycatcher)
Plate 27.6 *Ficedula subrubra**
Kashmira Laya Rathu-masimara කාෂ්මීර ලය රතු-මැසිමාරා

13 cm.
Forest edge, gardens, cultivations.
Common. Migrant. HC.

275. **SRI LANKA DULL BLUE FLYCATCHER** Plate 27.7
(Dusky Blue Flycatcher) *Eumyias sordida* *
Lanka anduru Nil-masimara ලංකා අඳුරු නිල්-මැසිමාරා

14 cm.
Endemic species.
Forests, gardens, well wooded ravines.
Common. BrR. HC and restricted humid locations in the LC mainly WZ.

276. **BLUE-THROATED FLYCATCHER**   *Cyornis rubeculoides**
Gela Nil-masimara ගෙල නිල්-මැසිමාරා

14 cm.
Male: deep indigo-blue above.
Brighter on forehead and supercillium.
Throat blue. Lores black. Breast reddish-brown.
Rest of underparts white.
Female: brown above. Reddish-brown rump.
Breast reddish. Throat buff. Rest of underparts white.
No white to base of brown tail.
Forest, with plenty of undergrowth, gardens.
Very rare. Migrant. LCDZ (mostly in the northern sector) and HC.

277. **TICKELL'S BLUE FLYCATCHER**   Plate 27.5   *Cyornis tickelliae* *
Laya thambilivan Nil-masimara ලය තැඹිලිවන් නිල්-මැසිමාරා

14 cm.
Forest near streams, undergrowth, gardens.
Common. BrR. All zones.

278. **GREY-HEADED CANARY FLYCATCHER** Plate 27.3
(Grey Headed Flycatcher)   *Culicicapa ceylonensis*
Hisa Alu-masimara හිස අළු-මැසිමාරා

9 cm.
Forest, gardens.
Common. BrR. HC and LCWZ (restricted locations).

279. **WHITE-BROWED FANTAIL** (Fantail Flycatcher)   Plate 27.9
Sudu Avanpendamara සුදු අවන්පෙදමාරා   *Rhipidura aureola*

16 cm.
Forest, scrub jungle, gardens.
Very common. BrR.
LC and hills up to 1500m (commoner in Uva Province, east and south-
east).

MONARCHINI

280. **BLACK-NAPED MONARCH** (Azure-blue Flycatcher)   Plate 27.8
Nil Radamara නිල් රදමාරා   *Hypothymis azurea* *

15 cm.
Female: duller and more brown than male.
Forest, gardens.
Common. BrR. All zones.

281. **ASIAN PARADISE FLYCATCHER**   Plate 27.4   *Terpsiphone paradisi*
Rahanmara   රහන්මාරා

20cm- (40 cm with tail streamer).
Forest, gardens.

Two subspecies, based on color differences of adult males.
Terpsiphone paradisi paradisi. (**Indian** or white phase).
Sudu Rahanmara (Suduredi Hora)   සුදු රහන්මාරා (සුදු රෙදි හොරා)
Forest, gardens.
Common . Migrant. All zones.
Terpsiphone paradisi ceylonensis. (**Brown** or dark phase).
Dumburu Rahanmara (Sivuru Hora)   දුඹුරු රහන්මාරා (සිවුරු හොරා)
Forest, gardens.
Common. BrR. LCDZ and HC, visitor WZ.

SYLVIINAE

282. **SRI LANKA BUSH- WARBLER**   Plate 28.7   *Bradypterus palliseri*
Lanka Rusi-raviya   ලංකා රුසි-රවියා

14 cm.
Endemic species.
Female: buff irides.
Young Male: irides pale reddish buff.
Young Female: irides white.
Forest undergrowth.
Rare. BrR. HC.

283. **ZITTING CISTICOLA** (Fantail-Warbler)   Plate 28.2
Rekhankitha Avan-raviya   රේඛාංකිත අවන්-රවියා   *Cisticola juncidis*

13 cm.
Marshes, paddy fields, tall grasses in damp situations.

Two subspecies, differentiated by color.
Cisticola juncidis cursitans **(Indian Fantail-Warbler)**.
"Pale".
Common. BrR. LCDZ.
Cisticola juncidis omalura **(Ceylon Fantail-Warbler).**
"Darker plumage".
Common. BrR. LCWZ and HC.

284. **GREY-BREASTED PRINIA** (Franklin's Prinia)   Plate 28.3
Frankalinge Priniya   ෆ්‍රෑන්ක්ලින්ගේ ප්‍රිණියා   *Prinia hodgsonii*

12 cm.
Female: breast band incomplete.
Marshes, grassland, scrub.
Common. BrR. All zones.

285. **JUNGLE PRINIA** (Large Prinia)   Plate 28.5   *Prinia sylvatica*
Maha Priniya   මහ ප්‍රිණියා

15 cm.
Grassland, scrub forest.
Rare. BrR. All zones.

286. **ASHY PRINIA**   Plate 28.4   *Prinia socialis*
Alupaha Priniya   අළුපැහැ ප්‍රිණියා

12 cm.
Grassland, scrub.
Common. BrR. All zones.

287. **PLAIN PRINIA** (White-browed Prinia)   Plate 28.6   *Prinia inornata*
Bama sudu Priniya   බැම සුදු ප්‍රිණියා

14 cm.
Grassland, paddy fields, scrub.
Very common. BrR. All zones.

288. **BLYTH'S REED-WARBLER**   *Acrocephalus dumetorum*
Blythge Pan-raviya   බ්ලයිත්ගේ පන්-රැවියා

14 cm.
Similar to Clamorous Reed-Warbler (289), but smaller.
Olive-brown above. Small supercilium.
Tail thin. Rump brighter.
Longish bill with base pinkish. Legs pinkish.
Marshes, paddy fields, scrub jungle.
Common. Migrant. All zones.

289. **CLAMOROUS REED-WARBLER** (Great Reed-Warbler)
Maha Pan-raviya   මහ පන්-රැවියා   *Acrocephalus stentoreus*

19 cm.
Greenish-brown above. Distinct whitish supercilium.
Underparts whitish to buff. Bill blackish
with pinkish gape. Legs pinkish.
Reeds, near water.

Two subspecies, indistinguishable in the field.
Acrocephalus stentoreus brunnescens **(Indian Great Reed-Warbler).**
"Paler, more rufous".
Status uncertain. Migrant. LCDZ.
Acrocephalus stentoreus meridionalis **(Ceylon Great Reed-Warbler).**
"Darker and smaller".
Common. BrR. LC.

290. BOOTED WARBLER
Ruk-raviya රුක්-රවියා

Hippolais caligata

11 cm.
Very much like Clamorous Reed-warbler (289) but
smaller, and with smaller bill. Above more
reddish-brown, tail less graduated and more
rounded with outer feathers pale- edged.
Reeds, gardens, hedges.

Two subspecies, indistinguishable in the field.
Hippolais caligata caligata (Booted Warbler).
"Tail usually less than 50 mm".
Very rare. Migrant. LCDZ.
Hippolais caligata rama (Syke's Booted Warbler).
"Tail usually more than 50 mm".
Very rare. Migrant. LCWZ.

291. LESSER WHITETHROAT
Sulu Gelasudda සුළු ගෙලසුද්දා

Sylvia curruca

13 cm.
Brownish-grey back, wings and head. Ear coverts grey.
Throat white. Tail blackish-brown. Outer feathers
white. Underparts white, tinged with buff.
Forest, scrub.
Very rare. Migrant. LCDZ.
[Hume's whitethroat - *Sylvia althaea althaea* is
included in this species. (Sibley & Monroe p 647).].

292. COMMON TAILORBIRD   Plate 28.1
Battichcha බට්ටිච්චා

Orthotomus sutorius

13 cm.
Garden, scrub.

Two subspecies, indistinguishable in the field.
Orthotomus sutorius sutorius (Common Tailorbird),
"plumage duller".
Very common. BrR. LC (HC up to 1500m)
Orthotomus sutorius fernandois (Highland Tailorbird),
"plumage darker".
Very common. BrR. HC.

293. **GREENISH WARBLER** *Phylloscopus trochiloides*
Kolavan Gas-raviya කොළවන් ගස්-රැවියා

10 cm.
Bright or dull green above. Distinct yellowish
supercilium. Dark streak through eye, cheeks
appear pale-yellow. Underparts
yellowish-white. Faint single wing bar.
Forest, gardens.

Two subspecies, indistinguishable in the field.
Phylloscopus trochiloides viridanus **(Greenish Tree-warbler).**
"2nd primary usually longer than 8th".
Rare. Migrant. LCWZ.
Phylloscopus trochiloides trochiloides **(Dull-green Tree-warbler).**
" 2nd primary usually shorter than 8th".
Very rare. Migrant. LCWZ.

294. **YELLOWISH-BREASTED WARBLER** Plate 25.8
(Green Tree-warbler)

Phylloscopus nitidus

Kola Gas-raviya කොල ගස්-රැවියා

10 cm.
The call is a soft chirp.
Forest, gardens.
Common. Migrant. All zones.

295. **LARGE-BILLED LEAF-WARBLER** Plate 25.7
Thuda loku Gas-raviya තුඩ ලොකු ගස්-රැවියා *Phylloscopus magnirostris*

12 cm.
The call sounds like the squeak of a swing.
Forest, gardens.
Common. Migrant. All zones.

TURDINAE

296. **BLUE ROCK-THRUSH** *Monticola solitarius*
Nil Gal-thirasikaya නිල් ගල්-තිරාසිකයා

23 cm.
Male: plumage dark blue, with a whitish and
brown scale pattern on body,
more pronounced in the belly region.
Female: grey brown with dark longitudinal
streaks. Rump barred blackish.
Pale wing bar distinct in flight.
Lower parts whitish cross barred with brown.
Forest undergrowth, rocky areas.
Rare. Migrant. LCDZ and HC.

162

297. SRI LANKA WHISTLING-THRUSH (Arrenga) Plate 29.2
Lanka Arangaya   ලංකා අරංගයා   *Myiophonus blighi*

20 cm.
Endemic species.
Female: browner, shoulder patch pale.
Around forest streams.
Very rare. BrR. HC.

298. PIED THRUSH Plate 29.5   *Zoothera wardii*
Gomara Thirasikaya   ගෝමර තිරසිකයා

23 cm.
Forest with undergrowth, gardens. Ground bird.
Rare. Migrant. HC.

299. ORANGE-HEADED GROUND THRUSH   *Zoothera citrina*
Hisa thambili Thirasikaya   හිස තැඹිලි තිරසිකයා

21 cm.
Head and underparts reddish-yellow.
Upperparts blue-grey. Wing patch,
vent and under tail coverts white.
Female: upperparts tinged with brown.
Forest undergrowth in damp conditions (ground).
Very rare. Migrant. All zones.

300. SRI LANKA SPOT-WINGED THRUSH Plate 29.3
Lanka thithpiya Thirasikaya   ලංකා තිත්පිය තිරසිකයා   *Zoothera spiloptera*

21 cm.
Endemic species.
Female: much lighter and paler.
Humid forests with undergrowth, forest edge.
Generally a 'ground bird'.
Common. BrR. All zones.

301. SCALY THRUSH Plate 29.4   *Zoothera dauma*
Pethigomara Thirasikaya   පෙතිගෝමර තිරසිකයා

24 cm.
Forest. A 'ground bird'.
Rare. BrR. HC (between 600-1500m elevation, commoner above 900 m).

302. EURASIAN BLACKBIRD Plate 29.6   *Turdus merula*
Kalu-thirasikaya   කළු-තිරසිකයා

25 cm.
Forest. Gardens. A 'ground bird'.
Very common. BrR. HC.

303. **INDIAN BLUE ROBIN** (Indian Blue Chat)   Plate 29.1
Indiyanu Neela-sittibichcha   ඉන්දියානු නිල-සිට්ටිබිච්චා   *Luscinia brunne*

15 cm.
Forest undergrowth.
Common. Migrant. All zones.

304. **ORIENTAL MAGPIE -ROBIN**   Plate 30.3   *Copsychus saulari*
Polkichcha   පොල්කිච්චා

20 cm.
Gardens, forest close to human habitation.
Very common. BrR. All zones.

305. **WHITE-RUMPED SHAMA**   Plate 30.2   *Copsychus malabaricu*
Vana Polkichcha   වන පොල්කිච්චා

25 cm.
Forests with undergrowth, gardens.
Very common. BrR. All zones.

306. **INDIAN ROBIN** (Black Robin)   Plate 30.4   *Saxicoloides fulicat*
Kalukichcha   කලුකිච්චා

16 cm.
Forest edge, gardens, scrub with open areas.
Very common. BrR. All zones.

307. **PIED BUSH CHAT**   Plate 30.1   *Saxicola caprat*
Gomara Sittibichcha   ගෝමර සිට්ටිබිච්චා

14 cm.
Forest, grasslands, open areas, bushes.
Very common. BrR. HC.

PARIDAE

308. **GREAT TIT**   (Grey Tit) Plate 32.2   *Parus majc*
Alu Tikirittha   අළු ටිකිරිත්තා

13 cm.
Forest, gardens.
Common. BrR. All Zones.

SITTIDAE

309. **VELVET-FRONTED BLUE NUTHATCH**   Plate 32.1   *Sitta frontalis*
Viluda alika Yatikirittha   විල්වුද අළික යටිකිරිත්තා

13 cm.
The habit of moving head down on branches is characteristic.
Forest (on tree trunks).
Common. BrR. All zones.

MOTACILLIDAE

310. **FOREST WAGTAIL**   Plate 30.8   *Dendronanthus indicus* *
Kala Halapenda   තැලෑ හැලපෙන්දා

16 cm.
Forest edge, paddy fields, open country, gardens.
Usually seen on the ground close to tree cover.
Common. Migrant. All zones.

311. **WHITE WAGTAIL**   *Motacilla alba*
Sudu Halapenda   සුදු හැලපෙන්දා

18 cm.
Hind crown and nape black, rest of
head white. Back and rump grey. Large white
patch or broad band on wings. Underparts white
with crescent-shaped black patch on breast.
Open country near water, paddy fields.
Very rare. Migrant. LC.

12. **WHITE-BROWED WAGTAIL** (Pied Wagtail)

Motacilla maderaspatensis

Maha gomara Halapenda   මහ ගෝමර හැලපෙන්දා

21 cm.
General plumage black. Distinct eyebrow,
large band on wing, outer tail feathers,
 belly and under tail coverts white.
Grey on flanks.
Female: browner.
Open country near water, canals, paddy fields.
Very rare. Migrant. LCDZ and HC.

313. **YELLOW WAGTAIL** *Motacilla flava*
Kaha Halapenda   තහ හැලපෙන්දා

16 cm.
Upperparts variable in colour. Underparts bright yellow, very distinct.
Open country, paddy fields, marshes.

Three subspecies (based on differences in upperpart color).

Motacilla flava thunbergi **(Grey-headed Yellow Wagtail).**
Hisa alu kaha Halapenda   හිස අළු තහ හැලපෙන්දා

Head, nape, and ear coverts, grey mixed brownish-green.
Faint white eyebrow.
Common. Migrant. All zones.

Motacilla flava beema **(Sykes' Yellow Wagtail).**
Sykege Kaha-Halapenda   සයික්ගේ තහ හැලපෙන්දා

Head pale bluish grey.
Clear white eyebrow and white malar streak.
Very rare. Migrant. LCDZ.

Motacilla flava melanogrisea **(Black-headed Yellow Wagtail).**
Hisa kalu kaha Halapenda   හිස කළු තහ හැලපෙන්දා

Head black. No eyebrow.
Very rare. Migrant. LCDZ.

314. **GREY WAGTAIL** Plate 30.5 *Motacilla cinerea*
Alu Halapenda   අළු හැලපෙන්දා

18 cm.
Throat of male becomes black in breeding plumage.
Open country near water, forest openings, paddy fields.
Very common. Migrant. All zones.

315. **RICHARD'S PIPIT** Plate 30.6 *Anthus richardi*
Richardge Varatichcha   රිවඩ්ගේ වැරටිච්චා

16 cm.
Open country, grass lands, paddy fields, cultivations.
Common. Migrant. All zones.

316. **PADDY-FIELD PIPIT** (Indian Pipit) *Anthus rufulus*
Indiyanu Varatichcha   ඉන්දියානු වැරටිච්චා

17 cm.
Very much like Richard's Pipit, but
shorter on the legs and smaller.
Open country, grasslands, paddy fields.
Very common. BrR. All zones.

166

DICAEIDAE

317. **THICK-BILLED FLOWERPECKER** Plate 31.5   *Dicaeum agile*
Thuda mahatha Pilalichcha   තුඩ මහත පිළිල්ලිව්වා

9 cm.
Forest, village gardens, cultivations.
Rare. BrR. LCDZ, occassionaly in HC.

318. **WHITE-THROATED FLOWERPECKER** Plate 31.4
(Legge's Flowerpecker)
Dicaeum vincens

Lanka Pilalichcha   ලංකා පිළිල්ලිව්වා

9 cm.
Endemic species.
Forest .
Common. BrR. LCWZ.

319. **PALE-BILLED FLOWERPECKER** (Small Flowerpecker) Plate 31.8
Kuda Pilalichcha   කුඩා පිළිල්ලිව්වා   *Dicaeum erythrorhynchos*

8 cm.
Smallest bird in Sri Lanka.
Forest, plantations, gardens.
Very common. BrR. All zones.

NECTARINIIDAE

320. **PURPLE-RUMPED SUNBIRD** Plate 31.2   *Nectarinia zeylonica*
Dam kati Sutikka   දම් කටි සුටික්කා

10 cm.
Bill slightly decurved, short.
Gardens, cultivation, forest.
Very common. BrR. All zones.

321. **PURPLE SUNBIRD** Plate 31.1   *Nectarinia asiatica*
Dam Sutikka   දම් සුටික්කා

10 cm.
Forest, gardens, cultivations.
Very common. BrR. All zones.

322. **LONG-BILLED SUNBIRD** (Loten's Sunbird) Plate 31.3
Lotenge Sutikka   ලෝටන්ගේ සුටික්කා   *Nectarinia lotenia*

13 cm.
Forest, mangroves, gardens, cultivations.
Very common. BrR. All zones (mostly coastline).

ZOSTEROPIDAE

323. **SRI LANKA WHITE-EYE** (Hill White-eye) Plate 31.6
Lanka Sithasiya ලංකා සිතාසියා *Zosterops ceylonensis*

10 cm.
Endemic species.
Forest, gardens, cultivations.
Very common. BrR. LCWZ (mid-elevations) andHC.

324. **ORIENTAL WHITE-EYE** (Small White-eye) Plate 31.7
Kuda Sithasiya කුඩා සිතාසියා *Zosterops palpebrosus*

10 cm.
Forest, scrub jungle, gardens, cultivations.
Very common. BrR. All zones (less in HC).

PLOCEIDAE

PASSERINAE

325. **HOUSE SPARROW** Plate 32.9 *Passer domesticus*
Ge kurulla / Chatakaya ගේ කුරුල්ලා/චටකයා

15 cm.
Human habitation.
Very common. BrR. All zones.

PLOCINAE

326. **STREAKED WEAVER** (Striated Weaver) Plate 32.3
Pan Wadu-kurulla පන් වඩ-කුරුල්ලා *Ploceus manyar*

15 cm.
The nest is built among reeds, and is not pendulous.
Reed beds, paddy fields.
Very common. BrR. LC (localised to southern coastal region).

327. **BAYA WEAVER** Plate 32.4 *Ploceus philippinus*
Ruk Wadu-kurulla රුක් වඩු-කුරුල්ලා

15 cm.
The nest is pendulous and usually built overhanging
ditches and water bodies.
Reed beds, paddy fields, close to water.
Very common. BrR. All zones (commoner in DZ).

ESTRILDINAE

328. **WHITE-THROATED SILVERBILL** Plate 32.7
(White-throated Munia)

Lonchura malabarica

Gela sudu Wee-kurulla ගෙල සුදු වී-කුරුල්ලා

10 cm.
Scrub jungle, grassland, cultivation, paddyfields.
Rare. BrR. LCDZ.

329. **WHITE-RUMPED MUNIA** Plate 32.6 *Lonchura striata*
Pita sudu Wee-kurulla පිට සුදු වී-කුරුල්ලා

10 cm.
Scrub, gardens, cultivation, paddy fields, forest.
Very common. BrR. All zones.

330. **BLACK-THROATED MUNIA** (Hill Munia) Plate 32.8
Kandukara Wee-kurulla කඳුකර වී-කුරුල්ලා *Lonchura kelaarti*

10 cm.
Gardens, plantation, grassland, scrub.
Common. BrR. HC.

331. **SCALY-BREASTED MUNIA** (Spotted Munia) Plate 32.5
Thith Wee-kurulla තිත් වී-කුරුල්ලා *Lonchura punctulata*

10 cm.
Grassland, scrub, paddy fields, gardens.
Very common. BrR. All Zones.

332. **BLACK-HEADED MUNIA** Plate 32.10 *Lonchura malacca*
Hisa kalu Wee-kurulla හිස කළු වී-කුරුල්ලා

10 cm.
Scrub, forest, paddy fields, reeds, grassland.
Very common. BrR. All zones, mostly in DZ.

PELAGIC AND INCIDENTAL SPECIES

PROCELLARIIDAE

CAPE PETREL
Daption capense

Keppa Pitaraliya කේ්ප්ප පිටරළියා

39 cm.
Black and white plumage. Clear white patches on upper side of wing.
Open ocean, coastal.
Single record. A specimen collected off the Gulf of Mannar
(Whistler, 1944: 290). Marine. Western sea and coast.

SOFT-PLUMAGED PETREL
Pterodroma mollis

Sumudu Raliya සුමුදු රළිය

34 cm.
Brownish-black upperparts. Underparts mostly white.
Breast band and flanks greyish. Belly streaked grey. Distinct face mask.
Open ocean, coastal.
Several sight records (De Silva, 1990:29). Marine. Western sea and coast.

BARAU'S PETREL
Pterodroma baraui

Barausge Raliya බරවුස්ගේ රළියා

38 cm.
Brown-black upperparts. Underparts, face, forehead and underwing,
white. Black marking around allula.
Open ocean, coastal. Sight record (CBCN, May, 1993:48).
Marine. Western sea and coast.

JOUANIN'S PETREL
Bulweria fallax

Jouaninge Pitaraliya ජොනින්ගේ පිටරළියා

26 cm.
Small size. Completely black-brown. Distinctive flight pattern.
Open ocean, coastal.
Single specimen. (Kotagama, 1980: 171).
Marine. Western sea and coast.

STREAKED SHEARWATER (White-fronted Shearwater)
Vatha sudu Diyalavakaya වත සුදු දියලාවකයා   *Calonectris leucomelas**

39-48 cm.
Brown above and white face streaks. Scale pattern on upperparts.
Whitish patch at lower back, above uppertail coverts.
Open ocean, coastal.
Two specimens. One collected in 1894 (Wait, 1931: 411) and the other
later (Phillips, 1978: 1). One sight record (De Silva, 1990:29). Marine.
Western sea and coast.

WEDGE-TAILED SHEARWATER (Green-billed Shearwater)
Palathudu Diyalavakaya   පලාතුඩු දියලාවකයා   *Puffinus pacificus**

43 cm.
Blackish-brown. Paler specimens present. Distinct wedge-shaped tail.
Open ocean, coastal.
Rare. Marine. Western sea and coast.

FLESH-FOOTED SHEARWATER   *Puffinus carneipes**
Palolpa Diyalavakaya   පළොල්පා දියලාවකයා

43-50 cm.
Dark sooty brown. Bill and feet flesh-colored.
Open ocean, coastal.
Three specimens procured so far. (Phillips, 1978:02; CBCN, May 1993:50).
Marine. Western sea and coast.

SOOTY SHEARWATER   *Puffinus griseus*
Dumbutuvan Diyalavakaya   දුඹුටුවන් දියලාවකයා

44 cm.
Blackish-brown with clear white line on underwing. Wings long.
Open ocean, coastal.
Sight record (De Silva, 1990:29). Marine. Western sea and coast.

SHORT-TAILED SHEARWATER (Slender-billed Shearwater)
Sihinthudu Diyalavakaya   සිහින්තුඩු දියලාවකයා   *Puffinus tenuirostris**

33 cm.
Uniform brown above, paler below. Short round tail.
Open ocean, coastal.
One specimen the only record (Phillips, 1978: 2).
Marine. Western sea andcoast.

AUDUBON'S SHEARWATER   *Puffinus lherminieri*
Audubonge Diyalavakaya   ඕඩුබෝන්ගේ දියලාවකයා

30 cm.
Blackish-brown upperparts. Underparts plain white.
Brown spreads down along neck to breast area.
Open ocean, coastal.
Sight record (De Silva, 1990:29).
Marine. Western sea and coast.

HYDROBATIDAE

WILSON'S STORM-PETREL   *Oceanites oceanicus*
Wilsonge Kunatu-raliya   විල්සන්ගේ කුණාටු-රැලියා

18 cm.
Brownish plumage. White rump. Square tail. Yellow foot webs.

Open ocean, coastal.
Common. Marine. Gulf of Mannar, western sea and coast
(May-November). See Phillips (1978:2).

SWINHOE'S STORM-PETREL (Ashy Storm-Petrel)
Alu Kunatu-raliya   අළු කුණාටු-රැලියා   *Oceanodroma monorhis**

20 cm.
Blackish to dark brown plumage. Forked tail. Black feet.
Open ocean, coastal.
Two specimens are the only records (Henry, 1971: 371; De Silva,1990:29).
Marine.

PHAETHONTIDAE

RED-BILLED TROPICBIRD (Short-tailed Tropicbird)
Ketiwala Gimvalaya   කෙටිවාල ගිම්වලයා   *Phaethon aethereus*

70 cm (tail 30 cm).
White plumage. Fine black barring on upper parts.
Narrow black band across wing.
Bright red bill. Long trailing tail feathers.
Open ocean, coastal.
One specimen (Phillips, 1978: 03) and several sightings.
Marine. Mainly western sea and coast.

WHITE-TAILED TROPICBIRD (Yellow-billed Tropicbird)
Hota kaha Gimvalaya   හොට කහ ගිම්වලයා   *Phaethon lepturus*

83 cm (tail 45 cm).
White plumage. No barring on upperparts.
Broad black band across wing. Yellow to reddish-yellow bill.
Open ocean, coastal.
Common. Marine. Mainly western and southern sea and coasts.

PELECANIDAE

GREAT WHITE PELICAN   *Pelecanus onocrotalus*
Maha sudu Pasthuduwa   මහ සුදු පැස්තුඩුවා

183 cm.
White plumage. Distinguished from the Spot-billed Pelican (2),
by larger size and large patch of bare facial skin. Primaries and
some secondaries black.
Br: rosy tinge to plumage and tuft of yellowish feathers on breast.
Lagoons.
One sight record (CBCN, May 1992:66). Vagrant. LCDZ.

SULIDAE

MASKED BOOBY — *Sula dactylatra*
Muvakalu Sulaviya   මුවකලු සුලාවියා

76-84 cm.
White plumage. Primaries, distal half of secondaries and tail black.
Yellow, reddish-yellow or darker feet (never red).
Open ocean, coastal.
Two specimens (Phillips, 1978: 4), few sightings.
Marine. Western sea and coast.

RED-FOOTED BOOBY — *Sula sula*
Rath-pa Sulaviya   රත්-පා සුලාවියා

70 cm.
White and brown plumage. Light and dark color phases present.
White or grey tail. Red feet.
Open ocean, coastal.
Two specimens are the only records (Henry, 1971: 365; De Silva, 1985).
Marine. Western sea and coast.

BROWN BOOBY — *Sula leucogaster*
Dumburu Sulaviya   දුඹුරු සුලාවියා

75 cm.
Chocolate brown plumage. White belly, wing lining and
undertail coverts.
Open ocean, coastal.
Common. Marine. All around Island.

FREGATIDAE

GREAT FRIGATEBIRD — *Fregata minor*
Maha Sahasiya   මහ සැහැසියා

Male: blackish-brown band on wings (median coverts).
Female: blackish-grey throat, white breast and sides of belly.
Open ocean, coastal.
Two specimens the only records (Phillips, 1978: 05).
Marine. Western sea and coast.

LESSER FRIGATEBIRD — *Fregata ariel*
Kuda Sahasiya   කුඩා සැහැසියා

Male: black with white patch on side of underwing (belly).
Female: black with white breast and sides of belly.
Open ocean, coastal.
Rare. Marine. Western sea and coast.

CHRISTMAS FRIGATEBIRD
Fregata andrewsi

Naththal-du Sahasiya නත්තල්-දු සැහැසියා

94 cm.
Black plumage. A distinct white belly patch.
Open ocean, coastal.
"Few (mostly dubious) sight records" (De Silva, 1990:30).
Marine. Western sea.

ARDEIDAE

GOLIATH HERON
Ardea goliath

S: Yoda Koka යෝධ කොකා

104 cm.
Largest of the herons. Grey upperback. Reddish brown crown and
underparts. Bill large. Heavy neck, drawn in during flight.
In flight: primaries appear black.
Marshes, lagoons.
Two specimens and two sightings. (Phillips, 1978:06) Vagrant, LCDZ.

GREAT BITTERN
Botaurus stellaris

Europiya Pan-koka යුරෝපීය පන්-කොකා

70 cm.
Thick neck. General body color brown with complex black
markings on upperparts. Dorsal half of neck and upperback barred.
Underparts pale with dark longitudinal streaks.
Black crown and narrow moustachial stripe.
Marshes, paddy fields, reed beds.
One specimen procured in 1985 (Gunewardena, 1985: 52-53), is the
only record. Vagrant.

CICONIIDAE

BLACK STORK
Ciconia nigra

S: Kalu Manawa කළු මානාවා

96 cm.
Black plumage. Belly, undertail coverts and axillaries white.
Red bill and legs.
Marshes.
A single sighting of two birds (Phillips, 1978: 9).
Vagrant. LCDZ.

WHITE STORK
Ciconia ciconia

Sudu Manawa සුදු මානාවා

102 cm.
White plumage. Black flight feathers. Red bill and legs.
Marshes.

Three sight records. Doubtful breeding record (Legge, 1880: 1120).
Vagrant. LCDZ.

ANATIDAE

GREYLAG GOOSE   *Anser anser*
Karalu Varataya   කාරලු වරටයා

84 cm.
General plumage gre-brown. Bill and feet pink.
Pale grey forewing in flight. Pale head.
Rivers, tanks, grasslands.
One specimen procured (only record) (Phillips, 1978: 11).
Vagrant. LCWZ.

COMB DUCK   *Sarkidiornis melanotos*
Kabalithiya   කැබලිතියා

76 cm.
Male: comb at base of upper mandible. Upperparts black.
Underparts white. Head and neck white, speckled with black.
Female: lacks comb and is paler. Lower back grey-brown.
In flight: broad, rounded black wings. Black bill and grey feet.
Marshes, tanks, paddy fields.
Rare. Status uncertain.
Formerly resident in Sri Lanka but now considered extirpated.
Present sightings are probably of migrant birds. LC.

GADWALL   *Anas strepera*
Gadwal Seruwa   ගැඩ්වාල් සේරුවා

51 cm.
Male: dark grey with brown head. Vent region, bill,
black and breast. Yellow feet.
Female: mottled brown plumage, yellow feet, yellow or
dull reddish-yellow patches on dark bill.
In flight: red-brown median coverts. Black greater coverts and
white speculum.
Marshes, lagoons, tanks.
One specimen procured (Phillips, 1978: 12) the only record. Vagrant.
LCDZ.

TUFTED DUCK   *Aythya fuligula*
Kudumbi Mada-seruwa   කුඩුම්බි මඩ-සේරුවා

40 cm.
Male: black plumage and white belly. Drooping crest.
Female: black of male replaced with dark brown. Short crest.
In flight: white band on secondaries shading to black of outer primaries.
Marshes, tanks, lagoons.

One specimen procured and one sight record (Phillips, 1978:13).
Vagrant. LCDZ.

ACCIPITRIDAE

EGYPTIAN VULTURE   *Neophron percnopterus*
Heenthudu Giju-lihiniya   හීන්තුඩු ගිජු-ලිහිණියා

61 cm.
White plumage with black primaries. Secondaries whitish above with
blackish band along tips of greater wing coverts. Facial skin yellow.
Strongly wedge-shaped tail. Head and throat with no feathers (naked).
Thick ruff round neck.
In flight: rather like the White-bellied Fish Eagle (47) but with smaller,
pointed, narrow wings.
Juvenile: white in the adults replaced by brown or buff.
Dry open country.
One specimen and one sighting (Phillips, 1978: 18) are the only records.
Vagrant. LCDZ (northern region).

LONG-LEGGED BUZZARD   *Buteo rufinus*
Dik pa Lassikussa   දික් පා ලැසිකුස්සා

61 cm.
Similar to an immature Brahminy Kite.
Plumage color highly variable, from dark brown through
reddish-brown, to sandy, pale brown.
Head, neck and breast almost white.
Black moustachial stripe sometimes present.
Long unfeathered legs.
In flight: Buzzard-like, with short neck. It is generally considered
difficult to identify in the field. (Ali & Ripley, 1969).
Forest.
Sight record (CBCN, January 1988:01). Vagrant.

BONELLI'S EAGLE   *Hieraaetus fasciatus*
Bonnellige Rajaliya   බොනෙල්ලිගේ රාජාලියා

64-69 cm.
Blackish brown upperparts. Paler, greyish tail.
Often greyish patch at base of primaries.
Irregular whitish patch on nape or upper back.
Underparts whitish, streaked with black.
In flight: white underparts. Leading edge of wing contrasting with
blackish wing lining and greyish flight feathers.
Tail with broad black subterminal band and several indistinct dark but
narrow bands.
Forest.
Only one recorded specimen (Phillips, 1978:16). Vagrant. LCDZ.

FALCONIDAE

RED-NECKED FALCON (Red-headed Falcon)   *Falco chicquera*
Hisa rathu Parisarikussa   හිස රතු පරිසාරිකුස්සා

31-36 cm.
Grey and white plumage with diagnostic reddish-brown head.
Open country, forest, scrub.
Sight record (CBCN, June 1986:22). Former records given by Legge
(1880:149) and Wait (1931:282). Vagrant. LC.

AMUR FALCON (Red-legged Falcon)   *Falco amurensis**
Rath pa Parisarikussa   රත් පා පරිසාරිකුස්සා

30 cm.
Male: upperparts dark grey except head and nape. Upper back and
upper wing coverts blackish. Brownish-red lower belly.
Orbital skin, bill, feet and claws reddish-yellow.
Female: slaty grey upperparts with narrow black bars.
Small moustache. Upper belly and flanks barred with black,
rest pale reddish-brown.
Juvenile: upperparts reddish-brown with narrow black streaks on head
and nape. Narrow black bars on rest of upperparts. Short tail.
In flight: white wing lining, blackish primaries and secondaries.
Open country, forest.
Two specimens procured in 1872 and 1932 are the only records (Phillips,
1978:20). Vagrant. LC.

TURNICIDAE

SMALL BUTTON-QUAIL   *Turnix sylvatica*
Punchi Bola-watuwa   පුංචි බෝල-වටුවා

19 cm.
Upperparts brown. Bright reddish-yellow patch on breast and black
spotting on side of body.
Scrub, grassland.
Sight record (CBCN, February 1978:07). Vagrant. LCDZ.

RALLIDAE

WATER-RAIL   *Rallus aquaticus*
Diya Reluva   දිය රෙලුවා

30 cm.
Long, slender. Upperparts buffy brown with black streaks.
Chin and throat white. Sides of head, neck and breast pale, slaty grey.
Yellowish-red bill. Sexes alike.
Marshes.
Three or four specimens procured remain the only record.
(Phillips, 1978: 22-23). Vagrant. LCWZ.

CORNCRAKE
Goda Keraliya   ගොඩ කෙරළියා

Crex crex

25 cm.
Yellowish buff with dark brown streaks above. Grey-blue stripe over
eye. Chin and throat whitish. Breast pale, ashy-grey.
Flanks and under tail coverts barred with reddish-brown.
Brownish-red wings in flight.
Dry grassland, cultivations.
Only two records of specimens (Phillips, 1978: 23). Vagrant. LCWZ.

CHARADRIIDAE

CHARADRIINAE

COMMON RINGED PLOVER
Mala Oleviya   මාල ඔලෙවියා

Charadrius hiaticula

19 cm.
General appearance similar to Little Ringed Plover (88) except
for the slightly larger, more robust build.
More yellow at base of bill. Lacks white line on fore crown.
In flight: distinct white wing bar.
Mud flats, wet sand flats, lagoons.
Few sight records (Phillips, 1978:27). Vagrant. LC.

LONG-BILLED PLOVER
Dik-hota Mala Oleviya   දික්-හොට ඔලෙවියා

Charadrius placidus

23 cm.
Similar to Common Ringed Plover, but differentiated by large size.
Bill proportionately longer and more slender.
Legs yellowish. Longish, graduated tail with blackish subterminal band.
In flight: wing bar white but inconspicuous.
Marshes, mud flats, lagoons.
Single sight record (De Silva, 1993:52-53). Vagrant. LCDZ.

ORIENTAL PLOVER
Peradiga Oleviya   පෙරදිග ඔලෙවියා

Charadrius veredus

24 cm.
Resembles a Golden Plover (86). Upperparts mixture of brown,
buff-brown and buff. Nape and crown brown. Feathers fringed buff.
Primaries dark brown. Underparts pale, brownish-buff throat and breast.
Rest dirty white. Legs and feet reddish-yellow.
In flight: no wing bar, entire underwing brown.
Marshes, mud flats, lagoons.
Single sight record-(CBCN, January 1994:02). Vagrant. LCDZ.

SOCIABLE LAPWING   *Vanellus gregarius*
Ranchu Kirala   රංවූ කිරලා

30 cm.
Ashy-grey and white plumage. Blackish-brown crown.
Brown line running from lores backwards through eyes.
Broad white supercilia and buffy forehead.
Black on tail tip and wing edge.
In flight: subterminal tail-band and primaries black.
Rump and secondaries white.
Open country.
Two sightings are the only records (Phillips, 1978:31). Vagrant. LCWZ.

SCOLOPACINAE

SWINHOE'S SNIPE   *Gallinago megala*
Cheena Kas watuwa   චීන කැස් වටුවා

28 cm.
Cannot be distinguished from Pintail Snipe (97) in the field.
In hand, tail feathers usually 20 or 22 in contrast to 26 or 28 in
Pintail Snipe.
Marshy areas, paddy fields.
Only two authentic records based on specimens (Phillips, 1978: 32).
Vagrant. LC.

GREAT SNIPE   *Gallinago media*
Maha Kas watuwa   මහ කැස් වටුවා

28 cm.
Darker and more heavily barred on lower parts and plumper than
common Snipe (98). Indistinguishable from other Snipe in the field.
In flight: more white on outer tail feathers; lacks white
band on secondaries; flight heavy, slower and more direct.
Marshes.
Very rare. Vagrant. LC (western area).

SLENDER-BILLED CURLEW   *Numenius tenuirostris*
Sihin thudu Kalikaya   සිහින් තුඩු කාලිකයා

39 cm.
Plumage similar to other curlews but whiter.
Distinguished by the absence of median and lateral crown-stripes.
Bill black with pink base.
Breast area with more distinct spots than other curlews.
Marshes, coast, mud flats, lagoons.
Sight record (CBCN: February1985:13). Vagrant. LCDZ.

ASIATIC DOWITCHER

Limnodromus semipalmatus

Asianu Sili-watuwa   ආසියානු සිලි-වටුවා

33cm.
Upperparts blackish-grey with pale fringes to feathers.
Breast and neck washed grey with fine brown streaks.
Belly white. Long, black, straight bill with enlarged tip.
Distinct eye stripe. Legs grey-brown. Breeding birds with white belly.
Marshes, mud flats, lagoons.
Sight record (CBCN, May 1981: 24; July 1982: 28b). Vagrant. LCDZ.

GREAT KNOT

Calidris tenuirostris

Maha nott Hinna   මහ නොට් හින්නා

23 cm.
Upperparts pale grey with narrow, blackish shaft-streaks and thin
whitish fringes. Underparts whitish.
Breast and upper belly streaked with blackish marks.
Breast-band formed by narrow streaks. Larger and longer body than
Red knot, longer bill, slightly down-curved. Legs dark green.
Marshes, mud flats, lagoons.
Few sight records. (CBCN, February 1981:17; May:24; 1984 Nov:38).
Vagrant. LCDZ.

RED KNOT

Calidris canutus

Rathu nott Hinna   රතු නොට් හින්නා

25 cm.
Scaly, ashy grey upperparts. Lowerparts white with faint spots or
streaks on neck. Whitish eyebrow. Short, straight bill.
Legs yellowish green and pale upper tail coverts and faint wing-bar.
In flight: seen in flocks.
Marshes, mud flats, coastal areas, lagoons.
One specimen and few sightings (Phillips, 1978:33). Vagrant. LCDZ.

WHITE-RUMPED SANDPIPER

Calidris fuscicollis

Nithamba sudu Hinna   නිතඹ සුදු හින්නා

22 cm.
Very similar to Curlew Sandpiper (117), but differs by having a distinct
white rump, a short straight bill with a yellowish-brown tinge at the base
and a more horizontal stance. Black legs. Breast streaked grey-brown.
Marshes, mud flats, lagoons.
Single sight record (CBCN, October 1980:50). Vagrant. LCDZ.

SHARP-TAILED SANDPIPER   *Calidris acuminata*
Ul penda Hinna   උල් පෙද හින්තා

21 cm.
Similar to Long-toed Stint (116), but larger.
Reddish-brown cap with black streaks on upper back.
Chin, throat, and abdomen white.
Foreneck and breast buffy and narrowly streaked.
Distinct border between breast and underparts.
In flight: pointed, white-edged tail feathers.
Marshes, mud flats, lagoons.
One specimen procured (Phillips, 1978:34). Vagrant. LCDZ.

DUNLIN   *Calidris alpina*
Dumbulu Hinna   දුඹුල හින්තා

19 cm.
Greyish-brown with less streaks on upperparts.
Pale greyish neck and breast.
Slightly decurved, black bill and short legs.
A hunched profile when resting.
Broad black line down center of rump, upper tail coverts and tail.
In flight: whitish wing-bar.
Marshes, mud flats, lagoons.
Many sightings since 1973 (Phillips, 1978:34). Migrant. LCDZ.

BUFF-BREASTED SANDPIPER   *Tryngites subruficollis*
Laya panduvan Sili-Hinna   ලය පඬුවන් සිලි-හින්තා

19 cm.
Blackish with feathers prominently bordered by buff.
Uniform dark rump. Buff underparts, throat and sides of face.
Distinctive upright stance. White underwing in flight.
Marshes, mud flats, lagoons.
One specimen (Norris, 1960: 330-331) and a few sightings (Phillips,
1978:35). Vagrant. LCDZ.

SPOON-BILLED SANDPIPER   *Eurynorhynchus pygmeus*
Handi-hinna   හැන්දි-හින්තා

15 cm.
Upperparts grey brown with dark shaft-streaks. White underparts.
Distinctly spatulate bill. Black legs.
Sweeps from side to side when feeding, a very distinctive movement,
rather like spoonbills.
Marshes, mud flats, lagoons.
Several sightings since 1978. (CBCN, February 1978:07). Vagrant. LCDZ.

PHALAROPINAE

RED-NECKED PHALAROPE

Phalaropus lobatus

Gela rathu Diya-watuwa   ගෙල රතු දිය-වටුවා

19 cm.
Streaked grey upperparts. White forehead and underparts.
Blackish eye-patch. Black, needle-like bill. Blackish-grey legs.
Often seen swimming.
In flight: broad white wing bar and dark outer tail feathers.
Marshes, mud-flats, lagoons.
Several sightings since 1978 (Dunnet, 1979: 215-216). Vagrant. LCDZ.

GLAREOLIDAE

COLLARED PRATINCOLE

Glareola pratincola

Javalihiniya   තරවැල් ජවලිහිණියා

25 cm.
Upperparts pale sandy brown. Darker primaries.
Folded wings extend beyond tail. Flight rather like a swallow.
Short legs. Resembles a tern when seated.
Breeding birds have a distinct black outline around buff throat patch.
Distinguished from the Oriental Pratincole (127) by being
paler and with the folded wings almost the length of tail or beyond.
Open country, beside marshes and lagoons.
Rare. Vagrant. LCDZ.

STERCORARIIDAE

BROWN SKUA   (Antarctic skua)

*Catharacta lonnbergi**

Antarctic Vulumbuwa   ඇන්ටාක්ටික් වුලුඹුවා

64 cm.
Gull-like, dark brown with various shades.
Heavy body, rounded tail.
In flight: broad rounded wing with large white patch at
base of primaries.
Open ocean and coastal.
About six specimens have been collected (Phillips, 1978: 38; De Silva,
1990:30). Marine. Mainly western sea and coast.

SOUTH POLAR SKUA

Catharacta maccormicki

Dakunu Vulumbuwa   දකුණු වුලුඹුවා

53-61 cm.
Similar to Brown Skua. Differentiated by smaller size.
Single specimen (Phillips, 1978:38), (De Silva, 1990:30). Marine.

POMARINE JAEGER   *Stercorarius pomarinus*
Pomarina Vulumbuwa   පොමැරීන වුලුඹුවා

51 cm.
Dark phase: dark brown.
Pale phase: lighter brown. Black cap. Yellowish-white lowerparts.
Under-tail coverts and breast band greyish brown.
In flight: long central tail feathers, broad wings with bright white
patches.
A single specimen (Wait, 1931: 395), a sighting
(Phillips, 1978: 38) and a few unconfirmed sightings.
Marine. Western sea and coast.

PARASITIC JAEGER (Arctic Skua)   *Stercorarius parasiticus*
Arctic Vulumbuwa   ආර්ක්ටික් වුලුඹුවා

48 cm.
Similar to Pomarine Jaeger but smaller. "Distinguished from it by
straight and pointed projecting central rectrices *contra* broad, blunt and
twisted" (Ali & Ripley, 1969, 3:20).
"Several (some dubious) sight records" (De Silva, 1990:30).
Marine. Vagrant.

LARIDAE

SOOTY GULL   *Larus hemprichii*
Dumbutuwan Galuviya   දුඹුටුවන් ගලුවියා

46 cm.
Upper back black. Breast and sides of neck blackish-grey.
Head blackish-brown. Distinct white collar.
Bill yellow with black and red bands at tip.
Feet green-yellow. No "windows" in primaries.
Coastal habitats.
Few sight records since 1993 (CBCN, January 1993:16). Vagrant. DZ.

YELLOW-LEGGED GULL   *Larus cachinnans**
Hurulu Galuviya   හුරුළු ගලුවියා

56 cm.
Grey upper parts (mantle), rest white.
Head and hind neck streaked with brown.
Bill yellow with red spot near tip. Feet flesh color to yellowish.
In flight: leading and trailing edge of wing white, wing tips black with
small white 'mirror' patch near tip in flight.
Sea-coast, rivers, tanks, lagoons.
(CBCN, June 1992:82-doubtful identification).Vagrant. LC.

COMMON BLACK-HEADED GULL *Larus ridibundus*
Hisa kalu Galuviya   හිස කළු ගලුවියා

38 cm.
NBr: mantle pale grey, rest of plumage white.
Head whitish with black patch behind eye.
Br: head dark coffee-brown to blackish. Bill and feet red.
In flight: leading edge of wing white with no 'mirror' near tip
of primaries. Long white wedge on leading edge of primaries
and black line on tips of primaries. Underwing dark.
Sea coast, estuaries, harbors, lagoons.
Several sightings since 1974 (CBCN, November 1974:41). Vagrant. LC.

SLENDER-BILLED GULL *Larus genei*
Sihin thuda Galuviya   සිහින් තුඩ ගලුවියා

42 cm.
Grey upperback. Rest of plumage white. Bill and legs dark red.
Bill with black tip. Elongate forehead and bill very distinct.
In flight: large white area along leading edge of outer upperwing.
Sea coast, lagoons.
Single sight record (CBCN, September 1978:50, De Silva, 1990:31).
Vagrant. DZ.

LESSER BLACK-BACKED GULL *Larus fuscus*
Kuda pita kalu Galuviya   කුඩා පිටකළ ගලුවියා

60 cm.
Br: plumage: head, neck, underparts and tail pure white.
Back (mantle) almost blackish. Reddish-yellow legs.
NBr: white head heavily streaked with brown.
In flight: contrasting white leading edge of wing and white
tips to black primaries.
Sea coast, lagoons.
Few sight records (Phillips, 1978:38-39).
Vagrant. Mainly western and south-western coasts.

WHITE-CHEEKED TERN *Sterna repressa*
Sudu-watha Muhudu-lihiniya   සුදු වත මුහුදු-ලිහිණියා

32 cm.
Upperparts grey. Underparts white. Black cap.
Entire plumage grey in breeding birds. Distinct white line below black
cap contrasting with rest of body. Non-breeding birds with white
forehead. Bill black with red base (red more prominent during breeding).
Legs red. Differentiated from Common Tern (137) by longer,
thinner bill and more black on head.
Sea coast, lagoons.
Single sight record (De Silva, 1990:31). Vagrant. LCDZ.

BLACK TERN *Chlidonias niger*
S: Kalu Kangul-lihiniya තල කාගුල්-ලිහිණියා

23 cm.
Br: black head, neck, breast and belly except lower belly and vent region.
Bill black. Legs blackish red.
NBr: grey and white with clear black shoulder patch and blackish cap
extending to ear coverts.
Sea coast, lagoons.
Sight records (De Silva et. al. 1992: 204-205). Vagrant. LCDZ.

BROWN NODDY (Common Noddy) *Anous stolidus*
Dumburu Nidi-lihiniya දුඹුරු නිදි-ලිහිණියා

43 cm.
Wedge-shaped tail. Completely brown except for whitish forehead and
pale grey crown. Bill and feet black.
Sea coast, marine islands.
Rare. Vagrant. LC.

LESSER NODDY *Anous tenuirostris*
Kuda Nidi-lihiniya කුඩා නිදි-ලිහිණියා

32 cm.
Very similar to Brown Noddy but distinguished from it by narrower
wings, blacker upperparts and darker underwing.
White (diffused greyish) on head more extensive, extending to lores.
Sea coast, marine islands.
Four specimens procured (De Silva, 1990:32). Vagrant. LC.

BLACK NODDY (White-capped Noddy) *Anous minutus*
S: Kalu Nidi-lihiniya තල නිදි-ලිහිණියා

34 cm.
Black plumage. Distinct white patch extending from forehead to nape.
Lores black. Bill black and thin.
Sea coast, marine islands.
Single sighting (De Silva, 1992, :175-176). Vagrant. LC.

COLUMBIDAE

PALE-CAPPED PIGEON (Purple Wood-pigeon) *Columba punicea*
Dampaha Maila-goya දම්පැහැ මයිලගොයා

40 cm.
Brownish bird with purplish-pink tinge on back, scapulars and
wing-coverts. Dark grey rump. Ashy-black tail. Underparts paler.
Male with a greyish white cap, which in the female is purplish ash.
Forest.
One specimen (Phillips, 1978:44) and a few sightings,
(CBCN, May 1983:18). Vagrant. LCWZ (possibly LCDZ too).

ORIENTAL TURTLE DOVE   (Rufous Turtle Dove)

Streptopelia orientalis

S: Rathu dumburu Tutura-kobeyiya   රතු දුඹුරු පුපුර-කොබෙයියා

33 cm.
Reddish-brown with brownish-red scaly patterned upperparts.
A "chess board" pattern on the side of the neck.
Pale grey tips to outer tail feathers.
Chin, center of throat, abdomen and undertail whitish.
Breast dark reddish-brown.
Forest, scrub.
Rare. Vagrant. All zones.

CUCULIDAE

COMMON CUCKOO   *Cuculus canorus*
Europiya Kokilaya   යුරෝපිය කෝකිලයා

33 cm.
Very similar to Indian Cuckoo (162), but differentiated by having a
yellow eye-ring. Grey upperparts, contrasting with a blackish tail.
The female has a color phase (termed "hepatic"),
entirely barred with black with upper parts brownish-red, throat
and upper breast buffy brownish-red and rest of underparts whitish.
Forest.
Very rare. Vagrant. All zones.

ASIAN EMERALD CUCKOO   *Chrysococcyx maculatus**
Maramini-koha   මරාමිණි-කොහා

18 cm.
Shining green above.
Male: lower parts green, the belly region white, barred with green.
White patch on base of primaries. Tail tipped with white.
Undertail coverts green with white bars.
Female: reddish-brown crown and nape, underparts mainly white,
reddish-brown on the throat. Flanks barred with brown.
Forest.
A single record based on the description of Brown (1776: 257).
Vagrant.

LESSER COUCAL   *Centropus bengalensis**
Heen Ati-kukula   හීන් ඇටි කුකුළා

34 cm.
Black plumage, chestnut wings. Tail feathers tipped with white.
Brown eyes, blackish bill. Female larger.
Grassland, marshes, forest.
One specimen (Wait, 1931: 220) and a single sighting (Phillips, 1978: 50).
Vagrant. LCDZ (north western region).

MEROPIDAE

EUROPEAN BEE-EATER
Merops apiaster

Yuropeeya Binguharaya   යුරෝපීය බිඟුහරයා

35 cm.

Upperparts yellow-brown. Underparts blue. Yellow cheek.
Reddish-brown crown, nape and back of neck.
Central tail feather elongated.
Open country, forest edge.
Few sightings since 1993 (CBCN, February 1993:23). Vagrant. LCDZ.

PICIDAE

EURASIAN WRYNECK
Jynx torquilla

Peradige Ka-kiriththa   පෙරදිග කෑ-කිරිත්තා

19 cm.

Upperparts silvery grey-brown, streaked, speckled and barred
with black and dark brown. Underparts whitish with arrowhead
markings, producing a fine, cross-barred pattern.
Tail with distinct three or four dark bands. Behaviour woodpecker-like.
Habitat?
Single sight record. (CBCN, December 1993:97). Vagrant. LCDZ.

HIRUNDINIDAE

SAND MARTIN
Riparia riparia

Karaval Ivuru-lihiniya   තරවල් ඉවුරු-ලිහිණියා

13 cm.

Upperparts smoky grey-brown, darker on wings and tail quills.
Underparts white with broad smoky grey band across breast.
Side of neck, throat and flanks light smoky grey.
Open country, near scrub, forest and water.
Sight records only (Phillips, 1978:62). Vagrant. LC.

PALE CRAG-MARTIN
Hirundo obsoleta

S: Sudumali Wahi-lihiniya   සුදුමැලි වැහි-ලිහිණියා

13 cm.

Upperparts pale brownish-grey. Wings and tail darker.
Underparts rusty cream color. Chin and throat streaked black.
Open country, near water, scrub.
Early record by Legge (1880:774); recent sighting by De Silva
(pers com). Vagrant. LC.

DUSKY CRAG-MARTIN *Hirundo concolor*
Anduru Wahi-lihiniya අඳුරු වැහි-ලිහිණියා

13 cm.
Upperparts dusky brown.
Underparts slightly paler than above. Chin and throat whitish.
White spots on all tail-feathers except the middle and outermost pair.
Short, square-cut tail.
Open areas close to water, scrub.
Sight records only (CBCN, January 1993:14). Vagrant. LCWZ.

WIRE-TAILED SWALLOW *Hirundo smithii*
Kooru penda Wahi-lihiniya තුරු පෙද වැහි-ලිහිණියා

13 cm.
Bright dark blue above. Crown brownish-red, underparts completely
white. Tail square. Very thin outer tail feathers, 3 cm or longer .
White lining on wing. Primaries blackish.
Usually near water.
Single sight record (Phillips, 1978:63). Vagrant. LCDZ.

STREAK-THROATED SWALLOW *Hirundo fluvicola*
Galpara Wahi-lihiniya ගල්පර වැහි-ලිහිණියා

14 cm.
Upperparts bright dark blue, becoming brownish on flight
feathers, rump and tail. Underparts buff-white, heavily streaked with
brown or black on chin, throat and more lightly elsewhere.
Crown dull chestnut. Tail slightly forked.
Open land, houses, near water.
Single sight record (Phillips, 1952:76). Vagrant. HC.

LANIIDAE

NORTHERN SHRIKE (Indian Grey Shrike) *Lanius excubitor*
Alu Sabarittha අළු සබරිත්තා

25 cm.
Grey head and upper back. Black tail with outer edge white.
Black wing with white spots. Rump white.
Black face mask distinct.
Open country, forest, scrub.
Sight records only (Phillips, 1978:64). Vagrant. LCDZ.

STURNIDAE

CHESTNUT-TAILED STARLING (Grey-headed Starling)
Alu hisa Sharikava අළු හිස ශාරිකාවා *Sturnus malabaricus*

21 cm.
Upperparts including head, silvery grey and brownish-red to grey.

Tail largely brownish-red. Wing-quills brown and grey.
Underparts, chin, throat and breast shiny-grey or pale brownish-red.
Rest of plumage bright brownish-red. Move in flocks.
Forests and gardens.
Few sightings since 1984 (CBCN, January 1984:01). Vagrant. LCDZ.

MUSCICAPIDAE

SYLVIINAE

RUFESCENT PRINIA $\qquad$ *Prinia rufescens*
Dumburu-rathu Priniya   දුඹුරු-රතු ප්‍රිණියා

11 cm.
Upperparts brownish-red to brown. Crown and nape ashy brown.
Lores and supercilium buff. In winter (migrant) plumage,
head and upperparts ashy brown. Underparts pale buff.
Pink mixed brownish-red on flank and lower belly.
Forest, scrub, among foliage and tall grasses.
Sight records only (De Silva, pers. com.). Vagrant. LC.

LANCEOLATED WARBLER $\qquad$ *Locustella lanceolata*
Lansa Palangeti-raviya   ලන්ස පළහැටි-රැවියා

13 cm.
Upperparts olive (yellow-green) - brown, streaked with black.
Supercilium pale yellow. Underparts very pale yellow.
Distinctly streaked on breast and flanks with dark brown.
Forest, scrub, among foliage and grasses.
Sight records only (Warakagoda, 1992 : 166-168). Vagrant. LC.

GRASSHOPPER WARBLER $\qquad$ *Locustella naevia*
Palangeti-raviya   පළහැටි-රැවියා

13 cm.
Upperparts olive (yellowish-green) - brown with broad dark brown
streaks. A pale narrow supercilium. Underparts whitish or pale
yellowish washed with buff on breast and flanks.
Lower throat often speckled. Undertail coverts very long, whitish with
broad brown shaft streaks. This species is distinguished from others of
the same genus by its plain brown tail without white tips and lack of
streaks on flanks and breast (Ali & Ripley, 1969:18:91-92).
Forest, scrub, grasses.
Sight record only (CBCN, December 1993:107). Vagrant. LC.

PALLASS' WARBLER (Pallas' Grasshopper Warbler)
Pallasge Palangeti-raviya   පලාස්ගේ පළහැටි-රැවියා   *Locustella certhiola*

13 cm.
Olive brown, the back streaked with dark brown and black.
Tail rounded, with white tips.

Crown streaked with grey and dark brown.
Pale supercilium. Underparts whitish, tinged with brown on the sides.
Buff under tail coverts. Undersurface of tail blackish with white tips.
Reeds, near water.
Two specimens (Phillips, 1978:79). Vagrant. LCWZ.

BROAD-TAILED GRASSBIRD (Broad-tailed Grass Warbler)
Palalpenda Thana-raviya   පළල් පෙද තණ-රැවියා   *Schoenicola platyura*

16 cm.
Reddish-brown above. Pale supercilium. Faintly crossed,
blackish-brown, rounded, broad tail.
Underparts whitish with buff on breast and sides.
Very faint buff supercilium. Black bill.
Tall grass patches, reeds.
One specimen (Legge, 1880:533) and two sight records (Phillips,
1978:79). Vagrant.

SAXICOLINAE

BLUETHROAT   *Luscinia svecica**
Gela nil Neela-sitibichcha   ගෙල නිල් නීල-සිටිබිච්චා

15 cm.
Brown above. Belly whitish and sides buff. Base of outer tail feathers
reddish-brown. Whitish eyebrow.
Male: reddish-brown throat patch bordered by blue, followed by a
black line, then white and finally red on breast followed by white belly.
Female: blue, replaced by buff. White and blackish streaks, on side of
throat give the appearance of a necklace.
Dense reeds, tall grass patches near water.
Few specimens and sightings (Phillips, 1978:82). Vagrant. All zones.

RUFOUS-TAILED SCRUB-ROBIN (Rufous Chat)
Dumburu rathu Chatasikaya   දුඹුරු රතු චටසිකයා   *Cercotrichas galactotes**

18 cm.
Sandy brown plumage. Distinct whitish supercilium. Dark line through
eye. Tail reddish-brown with a brown subterminal band and white tips.
Underparts creamy. Breast tinged with pale brown.Scrub jungles, open
country. Single specimen (Phillips, 1978:82). Vagrant. LCWZ.

PIED WHEATEAR   *Oenanthe pleschanka*
Gomara Kati-sithaya   ගෝමර කටි-සිතයා

15 cm.
Crown and nape white with brown-tipped feathers. Neck black.
Throat pale brown. Wings black. Rump and base of tail white.
Tail black and white with central feathers almost black giving a
T-pattern. Underparts from throat downwards dirty white.
Female: browner and paler than male, with buff supercilium,

T-pattern on tail present. Open forest, grassland.
Only two sight records (Phillips, 1978:83). Vagrant. LCWZ.

DESERT WHEATEAR
Oenanthe deserti

Kanthara Kati-sithaya   තාන්තාර කටි-සිතයා

15 cm.
Upperparts and crown sandy buff. Pale supercilium.
Uppertail coverts and basal half of tail creamy white.
Rest of tail brownish-black. Wings blackish brown.
Male: throat and sides of head black, rest buff-white.
Female: similar to male but greyer. Wing and tail paler than male.
Ear coverts brownish-red. Underparts whitish buff. Breast darker.
Open forest, grassland, rocky areas.
Sight records only (CBCN, May, 1986:22). Vagrant. LCDZ.

ISABELLINE WHEATEAR
Oenanthe isabellina

Isabellina Kati-sithaya   ඉසබෙලිනා කටි-සිතයා

16 cm.
Brown above. Pale supercilium and eye-ring.
Dark brown wings with buff edge. Base of tail feathers and upper
tail coverts whitish, rest of tail black. Creamy buff below,
darker on breast and sides.
Forest, open areas.
Only two sight records (Phillips, 1978: 83). Vagrant. LCDZ.

MOTACILLIDAE

YELLOW-HOODED WAGTAIL (Yellow-headed Wagtail)

Hisa kaha Halapenda   හිස කහ හැලපෙන්දා   *Motacilla citreola*

16 cm.
Head rich lemon-yellow. Sides of head, eyebrow and forehead dull.
Upperparts greyish. Two white wing-bands. Underparts yellow.
Open country near water, paddy fields.
Sight records only (Phillips, 1978:87). Vagrant. LC.

BLYTH'S PIPIT
Anthus godlewskii

Blythge Varatichcha   බ්ලයිත්ගේ වැරටිච්චා

15 cm.
Cannot be distinguished reliably in the field from
Paddy-field Pipit (316). Differentiated in the hand by the
triangular white pattern on second outer rectrice in Blyth's Pipit,
which is a narrow streak in the Paddy-field Pipit.
Open country, grassland, paddy fields.
Very rare. Vagrant. LC.

OLIVE-BACKED PIPIT
Anthus hodgsoni

Ruk Varatichcha රුක් වැරටිච්චා

15 cm.
Upperparts greenish-brown, streaked with darker brown.
Supercilium, double wing-band and outer rectrices whitish.
Underparts whitish to buff. Breast and flanks streaked with dark brown.
Open country, grassland, paddy fields.
Very rare. Vagrant. LC.

NECTARINIIDAE

CRIMSON-BACKED SUNBIRD (Small Sunbird) *Nectarinia minima*
Kuda Sutikka කුඩා සුටික්කා

8 cm.
Male: very similar to Purple-rumpedSunbird (374), but no green shoulder patch. Back and sides of head reddish. Underparts dull pale yellow.
Band covering breast broader. Back deep maroon-brown.
Rump purple, feathers tipped red.
Female: olive-brown with a crimson-brown rump.
Forest, garden, cultivation.
"Status uncertain - possibly a very scarce breeding resident in the low country wet and dry zones," (Phillips, 1978: 89).

PLOCEIDAE

PASSERINAE

CHESTNUT-SHOULDERED PETRONIA (Yellow-throated Sparrow)
Pingu-chatakaya පිඟු-චටකයා *Petronia xanthocollis*

14 cm.
Grey brown above. Tail and wings darker.
Reddish-brown shoulder patch. Two whitish wing bars.
Yellow patch on throat.
Rest of underparts pale grey-brown. Belly whitish.
Tail slightly forked. The female has a pale yellow throat patch.
Forest, scrub jungle, near villages and cultivations.
Two specimens from a "considerable flock" taken in
October 1876 is the only record (Phillips, 1978:90). Vagrant. LCDZ.

ESTRILDINAE

JAVA SPARROW
Ja-chatakaya ජා-චටකයා

Padda oryzivora

15 cm.
Crown, upper tail coverts, and tail black.
Cheeks and sides of neck white. Rest of upperparts, breast and wings grey. Belly and undertail coverts reddish-purple. Bill and legs red. Cities.
Introduced. Doubtful BrR. LCWZ.

GLOSSARY

Alula Four small feathers found on a bird's 'thumb'. They control airflow over the leading edge of the wing – the 'bastard wing'.

Axilla The area where the underwing joins the body. The feathers in this area are known as 'axillaries' or the armpit, e.g. Grey Plover.

Bar A fine, transverse mark.

Casque A helmet-like structure on the skull or bill, e.g. Malabar Pied Hornbill.

Cere Bare, wax-like or fleshy structure at the base of the upper beak, containing the nostrils, e.g. Cape Barren Goose, Peregrine Falcon, Budgerigar.

Coverts Small feathers hiding / protecting the bases of larger ones.

Culmen The ridge along the whole length or top of the upper mandible.

Ear tufts Feathers protruding from near ears, e.g. Sri Lanka Yellow-eared Bulbul.

Endemic Native to or peculiar to a particular or defined area.

Facial disc A bird's face, disc-like in form, being well-defined and comparatively flat, e.g. owls, harriers.

Flank Area on the bird's side, located directly below the forepart of the closed (folded) wing, e.g. heavy bars on Besra Sparrow-hawk.

Foreneck The whole front section of the neck.

Gape The fleshy corner of the beak which is often yellow, cream or pinkish in young birds.

Gular Of the throat. A gular pouch is distensible skin in the central area of the throat, e.g. Great Cormorant, Spot-billed Pelican.

Lamella A small layer of stiff hairs (membranes) on the inner edge of the bill, used to sieve food particles from water, e.g. ducks.

Lanceolate Spear-like in shape. Usually used in describing feather shapes.

Leading edge The front edge of a wing or flipper.

Lores Area between the bill and the eye, e.g. Little Tern.

Malar stripe Cheek stripe of, e.g. Brown-breasted Flycatcher.

Mandible The upper, or the lower, half of the bird's bill.

Mask Black or dark area which encloses the eyes and part of the face, e.g. Masked Woodswallow, Shrikes.

Mirror White circles (spots) in the primary feathers of gulls, e.g. Brow-headed Gull.

Nape The back of the birds's neck (and see Nuchal crest). e.g. Lesser Yellow-nape.

Nictitating membrane A third 'eyelid' that can be drawn across the eye from the nasal side for protection, lubrication and cleaning the eye. Some are translucent, some have clear central window so vision is not seriously impaired.

Nuchal crest 'Of the nape', e.g. Crested Tree-Swift. Nuchal crest is positioned on nape.

Orbit The space on each side of the skull filled by the eyeball.

Orbital ring A circular colour patch, fleshy or feathered, surrounding the eye, e.g. White-eye.

Pelagic Oceanic. Living far from land except when nesting.

Plumage The whole layer of feathers and down covering a bird's body.

Plume A long, showy, display feather, e.g. egrets.

Powder-down A fine white powder produced by feathers of some species (a) by disintegration of parts of some feathers or (b) by shedding cells which enclose portion of a newly growing feather's barbules, e.g. Spotted dove.

Rectrice The main feathers of a bird's tail.

Rictal bristles Stiff whisker-like protrusions about the base of the bill, e.g. Barbets.

Rump The squarish area between the lower back and base of the tail, e.g. Red-vented Bulbul.

Scapular Feathers which lie along the dorsal shoulder (base of the wing) of a bird.

Secondaries The inner flight feathers attached to the forearm.

Rachis The main stem (shaft) of any feather.

Speculum Iridescent, reflective dorsal patch on a duck's wing; contrasts with the rest of the wing. e.g. Garganey.

Superciliary The eyebrow stripe of some birds. e.g. Caspian plover, White-browed Bulbul, Indian Pitta.

Terminal 'At the end', e.g. white tail tips of Red-faced Malkoha.

Tertiary (feather) Row of inner flight feathers on a bird's 'upper arm';

Trailing edge The back or hind edge of a wing or flipper, e.g. Common Tern.

Underparts (ventrum) The chin, throat, breast, belly, underwing, flank, vent and undertail; the ventral surface of a bird.

Upperparts (dorsum) Frons, lores, face, crown, nape, mantle, back, upperwing, rump, base of tail, uppertail; the dorsal surface of a bird.

Vagrant A bird found in an area which is not its usual habitat having strayed there by mistake, e.g. disorientation, or forced by adverse winds.

Vent The cloaca – includes anus, oviduct and sperm duct openings. Also refers to patch of feathers around this. e.g. Red-vented Bulbul.

Wattle Paired fleshy lobes or appendages, often brightly coloured, hanging from the throat or neck of certain birds, e.g. Red-wattled Lapwing.

Wingspan The shortest distance between the wingtips; the greatest extent of the spread wings.

REFERENCES

Ali, S. & D. S. Ripley. 1969-1974. Handbook of the birds of India and Pakistan. 10 vols. Oxford Univ. Press, Delhi.

Brown, P. 1776. New illustrations of zoology containing... plates of new... birds, with a few quadrupeds, reptiles and insects, etc. London. 50 pl. with descriptive letterpress.

De Silva, R. I. 1985. A short note on the second record of a Red-footed Booby, *Sula sula rubripes* (Gould) from Sri Lanka. Loris, 17: 46-47.

De Silva, R. I. 1992. Black Tern- *Childonias niger*, in Sri Lanka. Loris, 19: 204-205.

De Silva, R. I. 1992. First sight record of Black Noddy - *Anous minutus*, from Sri Lanka. Loris, 19: 175-176.

De Silva, R. I. 1990. The seabirds of Sri Lanka (an annotated checklist). Ceylon J. Sci. (Bio. Sci.), 21: 28-33.

De Silva, R. I. & L. Perera. 1993. The Long-billed Plover - *Charadrius placidus*. Loris, 20: 52-53.

Dunnet, G.M. & S.W. Kotagama. 1979. Red necked Phalarope in Sri Lanka. J. Bombay Nat. Hist. Soc., 17:215-216.

Mayr, E. & W.J. Bock. 1994. Provisional classification of standard avian sequences: heuristics and communication in ornithology. Ibis, 136:12-18.

Norris, C.E. 1961. A new species added to Ceylon Avifauna: the Buff-breasted Sandpiper, *Tryngites subruficollis*. Loris, 8: 330-331.

Gunawardena, W. T. T. P. & D. P. Wijesinghe. 1985. The Eurasian Bittern - *Botaurus stellaris*: an addition to the list of Sri Lanka birds. Loris, 17: 52-53.

Henry, G. M. 1971. A guide to the Birds of Ceylon with 30 half-tone plates of which 27 are coloured and 136 black and white drawings. (2nd ed.). K.V.G. de Silva & Sons, Kandy, Ceylon. 457 pp.

Kotagama, S. W. 1980. First record of Jonanin's Petrel - *Bulweria fallax*, in Sri Lanka. Loris, 15:171.

Kotagama, S.W. 1986. කුරුල්ලන් තරඹමු [Let's watch birds]. Pubudu Prakashakayo, Colombo. 125 pp., 8 pl.

Legge, W. V. 1878-1880. A history of the birds of Ceylon. London. xlvi+1237 pp., 35 pl., 1 map.

Phillips, W. A. A. 1978. An annotated checklist of the birds of Ceylon (Sri Lanka). Rev. ed. Wildlife and Nature Protection Society of Ceylon. Colombo. 91pp. 2 pl.

Perera, D.G.A. & S.W. Kotagama. 1983. A systematic nomenclature for the birds of Sri Lanka. Tissara Prakashakayo, Colombo. 107 pp.

Sibley, C.G. & B.L. Monroe Jr. 1990. Distribution and taxonomy of birds of the world. Yale Univ. Press, New Haven. 1111 pp.

Wait, W. E. 1931. Manual of the birds of Ceylon. (2nd ed). Colombo Museum. 494 pp.

Warakagoda, D. 1992. The Lanceolated Warbler - *Locustella lanceolata*. Loris, 19: 166-168.

Whistler, H. 1944. The avifaunal survery of Ceylon, conducted jointly by the British and Colombo Museums. Spolia Zeylanica, 23: 119-321.

Index of Scientific names that have changed through taxonomic revision since Phillips (1978)

Phillips (1978)	Sibely & Monroe (1990)
Anthus novaeseelandiae richardi	*Anthus richardi*
Anthus novaeseelandiae malayensis	*Anthus rufulus*
Amaurorais fuscus zeylomicus	*Porzana fusca*
Apus melba bakeri	*Tachymarptis melba*
Bubo zeylonensis zeylonensis	*Ketupa zeylonensis*
Cacomantis merulinus passerinus	*Cacomantis passerinus*
Caprimulgus macrurus	*Caprimulgus atripennis*
Catharacta skua	*Catharacta lonnbergi*
Centropus toulon	*Centropus bengalensis*
Chlidonias lencoptera	*Childonias leucopterus*
Chalcites maculatus	*Chrysococcyx maculatus*
Collocalia fuciphaga	*Collocalia unicolor*
Coracira novaehollandiae	*Coracina macei*
Cypsiurus parvus	*Cypsiurus balasiensis*
Capella gallinago gallinago	*Gallinago gallinago*
Capella media	*Gallinago media*
Capella megala	*Gallinago megala*
Capella stenura	*Gallinago stenura*
Chaetura gigantea indica	*Hirundapus giganteus*
Capella minima	*Lymnocryptes minimus*
Clamator jacobinus jacobinus	*Oxylophus jacobinus*
Dapetor flavicollis flavicollis	*Ixobrychus flavicollis*
Esacus magnirostris recurvirostris	*Burhinus recurvirastris*
Egretta alba	*Casmerodius albus*
Erythropygia galactotes	*Cercotrichas galactotes*
Erithacus svecicus	*Luscinia svecica*
Egretta intermedia intermedia	*Mesophoyx intermedia*
Falco verspertinus amurensis	*Falco amurensis*
Glareola pratincola maldivarum	*Glareola maldivarum*
Glaucidium radiatum castanonotum	*Glaucidium castanonotus*
Glaucidium radiatum radiatum	*Glancidium radiatum*
Gelochelidon nilotica nilotica	*Sterna nilotica*
Himiprocne lonigipennis coronata	*Hemiprocne coronata*
Hypsipetes madagascariensis humii	*Hypsipetes leucocephalus*
Hypsipetes indicus	*Iole indica*
Hydroprogne caspia caspia	*Sterna caspia*
Ibis leuecocephalus	*Mycteria leucocephala*
Kitta ornata	*Urocissa ornata*
Lophotriorchis kienerii	*Hieraaetus kienerii*

Micropternus brachyurus	Celens brachyurus
Muscicapa rubeculoides	Cyornis rubeculoides
Muscucapa tickelliae	Cyornis tickelliae
Motacilla indica	Dendronanthus indicus
Muscicapa sordida	Eumyias sordida
Muscicapa parva	Ficedula subrubra
Monarcha azurea ceylonensis	Hypothymis azurea
Muscicapa latirostris	Muscicapa dauurica
Oceanodroma leucorhoa	Oceanodroma monorhis
Otus scops leggei	Otus sunia
Procellaria leucomelaena	Calonectris leucomelas
Phoenicopterus roseus	Phoenicopterus ruber
Picns myrmecophoneus	Picus xanthopygaeus
Pluvialis dominica fulva	Pluvialis fulva
Pomatorhinus schisticeps	Pomatorhinus horsfieldii
Procellaria carneipes	Puffinus carneipes
Procellaria tenuirostris	Puffinus tenuirostris
Podiceps ruficollis	Tachybaptus ruficollis
Rallus striatus	Gallirallus striatus
Sterna albifrons albifrons	Sterna albifrons
Sterna albifrons saundersi	Sterna saundersi
Tockus griseus gingalensis	Ocyceros gingalensis
Taccocua leschenaultii	Phaenicophaeus leschenaultii
Tringa terek	Tringa cinerea
Xenorhyachus asiaticus	Ephippiorhynchus asiaticus

පටුන

202

203

205

206

General Index

Scientific Index